*My* Dear Friend,

*I trust this book will be an inspiration to you in your spiritual walk with the LORD. There is nothing more exciting than seeing your faith, the size of a mustard seed, which GOD planted within your spirit, grow into a flourishing bush, bearing fruit, the answers, according to GOD'S promises that are "Yeah and Amen."*

*My desire is that this book will challenge you to learn to pray the Answer, instead of the problem. GOD is faithful to His Word; if you are willing to be careful what comes out of your mouth, remain steadfast and immovable in your faith walk; then you will see that GOD'S Word is HIS Will for your life.*

*Faith is not a religion; it is a relationship with our HEAVENLY FATHER that is acquired not in only a daily walk, but also in a moment by moment walk. It comes by surrendering everything in our life, by placing and leaving it in the FATHER'S Hand. JESUS said,*

*"Most assuredly, I say to you, whatever you ask the FATHER in MY Name HE will give you. Until now you have asked nothing in MY Name. Ask, and you will receive, that your joy may be full."*

*(John 16:23-24, John 15:16, Matt. 6:8 and Luke 11:13)*

*Sincerely,*

# Intercession: Touching God through His Promises

*Intercession: Touching God through His Promises*

By: Joseph D. Snook
Copyright © 2010
Revised 2022

# Handbook of Scriptural Prayers To Learn How to Become an Effective Intercessor

*"The effective fervent prayer of a righteous man avails much."*
*James 5:16*

By: J. D. Snook
Copyright © 2010
Revised 2022

**Gotham Books**

30 N Gould St.
Ste. 20820, Sheridan, WY 82801
https://gothambooksinc.com/

Phone: 1 (307) 464-7800

© 2023 *Joseph D. Snook.* All rights reserved.

No part of this book may be reproduced, stored in a retrieval system, or transmitted by any means without the written permission of the author.

Published by Gotham Books (November 9, 2023)

ISBN: 979-8-88775-599-1 (H)
ISBN: 979-8-88775-597-7 (P)
ISBN: 979-8-88775-598-4 (E)

Because of the dynamic nature of the Internet, any web addresses or links contained in this book may have changed since publication and may no longer be valid.

The views expressed in this work are solely those of the author and do not necessarily reflect the views of the publisher, and the publisher hereby disclaims any responsibility for them.

# DEDICATION

This book is dedicated to our LORD and SAVIOR, JESUS CHRIST.

*"The LORD gave the Word: great was the company of those that published it"*

*(Psalm 68:11)*

To all those who have a definite calling as or to be an Intercessor and who understand and know that intercession is always kept between true intercessors of the same mind and agreement according to the Promises of GOD; who know they have power over the enemy through the Word of GOD and HIS Promises; who are sensitive to the leading of the HOLY SPIRIT and know that when they are called to pray, it means **"RIGHT NOW!"**

To teach Intercessors how to pray effectively, and through these teachings and illustrations of prayer, how to effectively create intercessory prayers that are not included in this book; but willing to learn to grow by using one's faith; how to use GOD'S Word to battle and bind the enemy by using the Promises through the Power of Prayer.

# Table of Contents

Definition of Intercessors .................................................................. 1
Foreword .......................................................................................... 14
Introduction ..................................................................................... 18
Learning How to Become an Effective Intercessor ....................... 31
The Powerful Example of The LORD'S Prayer ............................ 39
The Apostles Creed ........................................................................ 43
What about Intercession for the Unbeliever? ................................ 45
Worship and its Importance in Preparing You to Receive the Word of GOD ............................................................................................ 47
Prayers of Praise ............................................................................. 55
Personal Confessions ..................................................................... 57
Examples of INTERCESSION Prayers of Faith: .......................... 60
For our President and the Leaders in our Government ................. 60
For Nations and Continents ........................................................... 64
For the School Systems (Authority, Children and Parent) ........... 66
For the Body of CHRIST ............................................................... 70
Pray for Jerusalem .......................................................................... 73
For Ministers and Ministries .......................................................... 76
For Missionaries ............................................................................. 79
For Meetings, Seminars and Bible Studies ................................... 82
Prosperity for Ministering Servants .............................................. 84
To Be GOD-inside Minded ............................................................ 87
For GOD'S Word and an Accurate Prayer Life ............................ 89
To Rejoice in the LORD ................................................................ 92
To Walk in GOD'S Wisdom and His Perfect Will ....................... 94
To Walk in Love ............................................................................. 97

| | |
|---|---|
| To Watch What You Say | 99 |
| To Live Free from Worry | 101 |
| From Corrupt Companions | 103 |
| From Satan and His Demonic Forces Regarding: (Alcoholism, Gambling, Narcotics, the Occults, etc.) | 105 |
| Deliverance of Loved Ones from Cults | 109 |
| From Bad Habits | 113 |
| From Depression | 115 |
| To Receive JESUS as SAVIOR and LORD | 117 |
| For Salvation in General | 118 |
| For Specific Salvation | 120 |
| To Receive the Infilling of the HOLY SPIRIT | 122 |
| A Confession of Forgiveness for the Believer | 123 |
| Renewed Fellowship | 125 |
| For Boldness and Authority | 127 |
| On Improving Communication with a Loved One | 129 |
| For Those Involved in Court Cases | 131 |
| For Employment | 133 |
| For Finding Favor with Others | 135 |
| For Safety | 137 |
| For Singles Trusting GOD for a Mate | 139 |
| For a Spirit-controlled Life | 141 |
| For Victory over Fear | 143 |
| For Victory Over Gluttony | 145 |
| For Health and Healing | 148 |
| For Unknown Types of Diseases and Cancer | 151 |
| Intercession for the Handicapped | 155 |
| For Children and Parents | 159 |
| For the Home | 162 |
| For Our Mates | 164 |

For a Harmonious Relationship (Union) ....................................... 166
For Compatibility in the Home (Union) ...................................... 168
Intercession for a Troubled Relationships ................................... 170
For the 100-fold Return ................................................................ 172
Prosperity for You and Others .................................................... 174
A Dedication for Your Tithes ...................................................... 176
References .................................................................................. 178
Notes: .......................................................................................... 179

# Definition of Intercessors

An intercessor is a prayer warrior. In order to be an intercessor, you MUST have a calling or commitment to adhere to the quickness of the prompting of the HOLY SPIRIT. To be quick to begin interceding where ever you are; this is where the Gift, that the HOLY SPIRIT has blessed us with, which is often considered the lesser gift, but as an intercessor, it is one of the most powerful gifts given by the HOLY SPIRIT called "**tongues**" or as I use the term "**Heavenly Language**."

*"²⁶ In the same way the SPIRIT [comes to us and] helps us in our weakness. We do not know what prayer to offer or how to offer it as we should, but the SPIRIT Himself [knows our need and at the right time] intercedes on our behalf with sighs and groanings too deep for words [those are the moments when we use our Heavenly Language to intercede]. ²⁷ And HE who searches the hearts knows what the Mind of the SPIRIT is, because the SPIRIT intercedes [before GOD] on behalf of GOD'S people in accordance with GOD'S [perfect] Will."*

*Romans 8:26-27 – (The New Amplified Bible)*

I am very much aware that many Christian denominations do not believe in the use of this gift, but it is listed in the Word of GOD and it does not say that it was for the days of old; nor does it say that it is a useless gift for today. From my experience as an intercessor, it is quite clear in this present day that any true intercessor would understand this as GOD'S Truth. The reason is when we are called, prompted or quickened to flow into intercession, GOD may only give us a name, but not a situation, there are other times when we don't even know the name or the situation, we just know to begin to pray in the Spirit and the reason may be because the situation is a delicate situation; or GOD may not want certain words to be mentioned in order for GOD to thwart the enemy's plan. Keep in mind that every time we use our native language; Satan, being the prince of this world can hear and understand, but he cannot under the Heavenly Language. Therefore, he will do anything to hinder your prayer life, including Christians (brothers and sisters) by interfering and giving room for them to speak negatively regarding what was said or prayed. Agreement in prayer is imperative, especially if you are praying with other intercessors, but as you pray in the Spirit, then you may understand only if the HOLY SPIRIT gives you understanding; otherwise, only the Great Intercessor—JESUS CHRIST will present the need to the FATHER.

**(18) "Assuredly, I say to you, whatever you bind on earth will be bound in heaven, and whatever you loose on earth will be loosed in heaven.**

**(19) "Again, I say to you if two of you agree on earth concerning anything that they ask, it will be done for them by my FATHER in heaven."** *(Matthew 18: 18-19)*

Also, keep in mind, being an intercessor is a lonely ministry, but it is also a very important and rewarding ministry, especially as you see the answers to prayer come into being, praying with powerful faith for those things which are not, as though they were. It is a lonely ministry because it is a ministry that you cannot be sharing information with others. It is the true work of your faith according to the Promises of GOD that bring forth HIS answers to prayer. The less you share about the problems, the more you will see the rewards to the answers through intercession prayers.

Another important factor is when you ask GOD once; you will learn quickly, there is no need to keep asking again and again. That is why the Word of GOD continually tells us to give "**Thanks**." As parents, we get annoyed when our children keep asking the same question over and over again, especially when we have given them a verbal answer. How much more can you understand why our FATHER, said to ask, in JESUS' Name, and to give thanks for the answer?

Regarding speaking in your "**Heavenly Language**;" which many times happens in the in the middle of the night. GOD will put a person on your mind, even though you have no idea what they are going through at that moment; but keep in mind that GOD is all-knowing, so HE completely knows of individuals situations and what is happening within their lives, that is why HE has prompted you to pray, or to "**stand in the gap**" for someone else; but again, we often don't know what the problem is. This is where the lesser of gift of the Heavenly Language is so important for an intercessor, because you are not only praying in the Spirit, but you are also praying the total Will of GOD to come forth. Praying in the Spirit are not words that GOD will misunderstand regarding the situation; but more important, the Heavenly Language cannot be understood or interpreted by the enemy to interfere with

GOD'S master plan, yet you are interceding exactly what the FATHER'S Will is to be accomplished.

The following scriptures are referring to the entire GOD given Spiritual Gifts, especially mentioned in I Corinthians 11 and 12.

*(I Corinthians 11:4-10) "There are diversities of gifts, but the same Spirit.*

*(5) There are differences of ministries, but the same LORD.*

*(6) And there are diversities of activities, but it is the same GOD who works all in all.*

*(7) But the manifestation of the Spirit is <u>given to each one</u> for the <u>profit of all</u>:*

*(8) for to one is given the <u>word of wisdom</u> through the Spirit, to anther the <u>word of knowledge</u> through the same Spirit,*

*(9) to another <u>faith</u> by the same Spirit, to anther <u>gifts of healings</u> by the same Spirit,*

*(10) to another the <u>working of miracles</u>, to another <u>prophecy</u> (prophecy in the N.T. is ALWAYS forth telling, never foretelling; foretelling was for the prophets in the O.T.), to anther <u>discerning of spirits</u>, to anther <u>different kinds of tongues</u>, to anther <u>the interpretation</u> of tongues."*

Paul wrote these Scriptures as spiritual instructions by the HOLY SPIRIT for the setting of a body jointed together in worship (or church setting), but as an individual all these gifts should be a desire to be part of their life or why would be we admonished to desire the gifts of the Spirit? In verses 8 through 10, these underlined gifts are especially needed for an intercessor and/or if you are called to be an intercessor, you should desire these gifts: (1) The **word of wisdom**, because it is the HOLY SPIRIT who prompts you to intercede for individuals in the Body of CHRIST (that does not mean you need to know the problem, you need to know the scriptures concerning wisdom – by coming to know and learn the book of Proverbs which is filed with GOD'S Wisdom); (2) The **word of knowledge**, is used by the HOLY SPIRIT to forbid the problem to be known by the enemy so he has no way of hindering an individual's life, or so the information is not to be shared with anyone else except the person with whom is having the problem (how will you know if you should speak to them? You will know when they come to you for counsel, they will bring it up; (3) the gift of **faith** is very important as an intercessor, not only for yourself, but the HOLY SPIRIT, Who may instruct you to lay hands on that individual to allow the anointing of this gift to flow into their being and encourage the same measure of faith that GOD has given to every individual. Yet many times, the enemy may try to belittle them or make them feel as though they are not worthy, or to play with their mind making them think they lack the faith (the gift of faith is an anointing that breaks the working of the enemy from discouraging any individual, this is when the HOLY SPIRIT may also prompt you to share wisdom and/or disclose the person's situation, but those words of disclosure will always be words of a minimum, never the whole tale); (4) this is why the gift of the **discerning of spirits** is essential as an intercessor , you need to be aware of the different spirits and cohorts that the enemy has in this world that are interfering with another individual (remember that Satan is the prince of this world, DO NOT be deceived that you are dealing just with Satan, but with his a whole army of demonic cohorts and fallen angels, and, yes, he may even use other Christians – brothers and sisters, to discourage an individual), this again, is why it is important for an intercessor to desire the Gifts of the HOLY SPIRIT, you need to be sensitive to the Voice of the HOLY SPIRIT as HE may prompts you to speak in private with another believer, especially if Satan is using them to discourage other people (also, keep in mind, when I use the word "*people*" it can be adults, adolescents or children, I have seen many adults put children down, which goes against the Scriptures especially with the example of JESUS blessing the children and what did HE say? (Matthew 19:14) "*Let the little children come to Me, and do not forbid them; for of such is the Kingdom of Heaven.*" JESUS also said, (Matthew 21:16) "…*Yes. Have you never read* (referring to Psalms 8:2), …*Out of the mouth of babes and nursing infants you have perfected praise?*"; (5) the gift of **tongues** is absolutely needed as an intercessor, the HOLY SPIRIT may prompt us to pray for an individual, but when HE does not give us any inkling of what or how to pray, this is where praying in the Spirit lead us to pray in tongues, the Heavenly Language, that only GOD, the FATHER, SON and HOLY SPIRIT understand and again, take **NOTE**: <u>Satan cannot understand the Heavenly Language</u> – so you are blocking Satan's every maneuver to hinder an individual's life by praying in the Spirit, (Romans 8:26) "*Likewise the SPIRIT also helps in our weaknesses. For we do not know what we should pray for as we ought, but the SPIRIT HIMSELF* *makes intercession* [within our own spirit] *for us with groanings which cannot be uttered (or understood)*".

The other four gifts are healings, miracles, prophecy, and interpretations of tongues. Let's address these last four gifts. Healing is a gift that I have seen go to the individuals that Satan may use to cause you to think you are special before GOD, or it may sometimes cause us to lose sight and humble ourselves, thinking we are better than other, so in those moments we need to be careful in our actions and realize no one is better than anyone else; so the spirit of being boastful is having a haughty spirit which is not from GOD. Therefore, be careful and stay sensitive and humble with all the Gifts given by the HOLY SPIRIT. As children of GOD, every individual Created by GOD is special in HIS Eyes, for HE loves everyone and therefore, we should never allow that spirit to make us think we are better than other person; GOD has called us to humble ourselves for HIM and others. Regarding healing never assume to lay hands on a person for their healing or even for to use the gift of faith, until the HOLY SPIRIT prompts you to do so. You will find through experience that if a person is NOT ready or spiritually prepared by the HOLY SPIRIT to receive what GOD has for them, and you do lay your hands on them, you will sense the spiritual energy "bounce back into you;" at that point flow out of you, but if it "bounce back into you;" at that point you will know they have not received GOD'S miraculous blessing due to the lack of faith.

The gift of miracles is also another unique gift, but needs to be used in the same manner as in healing and it is also a gift that should always be used with humility, giving GOD all the Glory. We are only

HIS vessels to touch and love people who are hurting; and who desire GOD'S Love.

The gift of prophecy is a gift that definitely needs to be used only by the leading of the HOLY SPIRIT and in the New Testament it is really forth telling what has already been recorded within the Word of GOD and as they prophecy it must always come in line with the Word of GOD. The person in the New Testament who had the ability to be use with prophesy was John, when he was on the Isle of Patmos as he spoke forth, prophesying regarding the Book of Revelation. The Old Testament Prophets were given the ability to prophesy or to speak forth those things that were to come into being in the future.

I have seen people who have the New Testament gift resolving problems, and I have also seen them misuse it creating division and havoc, both within the body and individually. I have found GOD'S assurance when using this gift, especially with individuals; it was usually when the individual came to them for counsel. You will already know because the HOLY SPIRIT has prepared you, just as HE has prepared them. Therefore, you should never bombard an individual to prophecy when they have not been prepared by the HOLY SPIRIT, and it will never be by the laying on of hands unless for any reason the HOLY SPIRIT would specifically instruction, or you are basically getting ahead of the HOLY SPIRIT; which will end up being rejected and not received and you will end up giving the enemy the open door to thwart what GOD meant to work for good. It is always important to WAIT on the LORD ("*...wait on the LORD and you will be renewed with strength*") until the HOLY SPIRIT prepares the recipient to accept what needs to be said, in order to receive a profound statement or a rebuke or correct which will spiritually strengthen the person. Now not all prophesy is pointing out the negative area in a person's life, prophesy is mostly used to encourage people in their work of faith or to conform what they have already been enlightened by the HOLY SPIRIT to move forward to receive GOD'S blessings, it also points a person in the right direction, especially if they are at a fork in the road and are unsure of which way to go. I often point out that there are always pros and cons, but if you listen to the LORD, HE will give you the spirit of agreement, that is why JESUS said, *"(29) Take my yoke upon you and learn from ME, for I am gentle and lowly in heart, and you will find rest for your souls [minds]. (30) For MY yoke is <u>easy</u> and MY <u>burden</u> is light."* (Matthew 11:29-30) A yoke is a wooden crosspiece that is fastened over the necks of two animals and attached to a plough or cart so they will pull together in unison; keep in mind that the yoke is for two (2), JESUS and you, so you can walk in unison with the together. Also, take notice to the underlined words, "**easy**" and "**burden**"; this world needs to know that GOD'S promises provide an easier way to accomplish what GOD wants to bring forth in your life. We often hear, "When the door is closed, a window will open," but keep in mind, you can walk through a door, but you may have to crawl out of a window, which is easier? Prophesying always points you to the easy way, although it does not mean that you will not have obliges to face, but through them you will have success.

Let's address "interpretation of tongues." I feel this happens most of the time in the Body of a church setting, there will be one who will bring forth the utterance of tongues and then another who will bring forth the interpretation of the message in tongues by the HOLY SPIRIT. Although, as an intercessor, there will be those occasions when the HOLY SPIRIT will disclose or interpret what you have prayed in the Spirit. Why? Only GOD can answer that, but my thought on this matter is when we intercede in the Spirit in our own setting it is at that point when we are often in a face to face spiritual warfare with the enemy. Once the enemy is bound in that particular area, the HOLY SPIRIT may give you understanding to effectively use the Promises of GOD'S Word to "**spiritually handcuff**" the enemy in that event. This is another reason why Paul encourages us to put on the whole Amor of GOD.

*Ephesians 6:10-11 and 14-17 – (The New Amplified Bible)*

"*10 In conclusion, be strong in the LORD [draw your strength from HIM and be empowered through your Union/ Relationship with HIM] and in the Power of HIS [boundless] Might. 11 Put on the Full Armor of GOD [for HIS precepts are like the splendid Armor of a heavily-armed soldier], so that you may be able to [successfully] stand up against all the schemes and the strategies and the deceits of the devil.*"

"*14 So stand firm and hold your ground, having tightened the Wide Band of Truth (personal integrity, moral courage) around your waist and having put on the Breastplate of Righteousness (an upright heart), 15 and having Strapped on your Feet the Gospel of PEACE in preparation [to face the enemy with firm-footed stability and the readiness produced by the Good News]. 16 Above all, lift up the [protective] Shield of Faith with which you can extinguish all the flaming arrows of the evil one.*

*17 And take the Helmet of Salvation, and the Sword of the SPIRIT [the Two-edged Sword], which is [speaking forth] the WORD of GOD."*

Another term for an Intercessor is a **Warrior**, since we are constantly prompted to intercede for so many different situations, when you are entering into spiritual warfare against the enemy and his entire foe; we move forward being fully prepared by knowing the Word of GOD, so we can speak the Word so HIS Power goes forth, in the Name of JESUS, to dissipate the enemy. The Word of GOD tells us, when the enemy comes against you one way, HE will cause the enemy to flee in seven different ways. I will go deeper into this subject later regarding intercession.

*(Romans 12:3-8) "For I say, through the grace given to me, to everyone who is among you, not to think of himself more highly than he ought to think, but to think soberly, as GOD has dealt to each one of you a measure of faith.*

*(4) For as we have many members in one body, but all the members do not have the same function,*

*(5) so weak, being many, are one body in CHRIST, and individually members of one another.*

*(6) Having been gifts differing according to the grace that is given to us, let us use them: if prophecy, let us prophesy in proportion to our faith;*

*(7) or ministry, let us use it in our ministering; he who teaches,*

*in teaching;*

*(8) he who exhorts, and exhortation; he who gives, with liberality; he who leads, with diligence; he who shows mercy, with cheerfulness."*

Again, as intercessors, the more you follow the Scriptures, the more people who are call into this ministry will desire all of the Spiritual Gifts given from the HOLY SPIRIT:

*(Ephesians 4:4-10) "**4** **There is one body** [of believers] **and one Spirit—just as you were called to one Hope when called** [to Salvation] **5 one LORD, one faith, one baptism, 6 one GOD and FATHER of us all Who is** [sovereign] **overall and** [working] **through all and [living] in all. 7 Yet grace** [GOD'S undeserved favor] **was given to each one of us** [not indiscriminately, but in different ways] **in proportion to the measure of CHRIST'S** [rich and abundant] **gift. 8 Therefore it says, "When HE ascended on high, HE led captivity captive, And HE bestowed gifts on men." 9 (Now this expression, "HE ascended," what does it mean except that HE also had previously descended** [from the heights of Heaven] **into the lower parts of the earth? 10 HE who descended is the very same as HE who also has ascended high above all the Heavens, that HE** [HIS presence] **might fill all things** [that is, the whole universe]).*

Therefore according to Ephesians 4:12, keep in mind this is referring to all of the gifts of the HOLY SPIRIT:

*(Ephesians 4:12-16)* ***(gifts of the Spirit are) "for the equipping of the saints for the work of ministry, for the edifying of the body of CHRIST."***

***(13) till we all come to the unity of states and of the knowledge of the son of GOD, to a perfect man, to the measure of the statute of the fullness of CHRIST;***

***(14) that we should no longer be children, tossed two at 40 and carried about with every wind of, by the trickery of men, and exciting craftiness of deceitful plotting, (15) but, speaking the truth in love, may grow up in all things into HIM who is the head – CHRIST – (16) from whom the whole body, joined and knit together by what every joint supplies, according to the effective working by which every part does its share, causes growth of the body for the edifying of itself in love."***

# Foreword

The prayers in this book are to be used by you for yourself and as you intercede for others. They are a matter of the heart. The Gifts are for your purpose; therefore, it would be wise to meditate and feed the Word of GOD to fill your inner spirit. Always allowing the HOLY SPIRIT to bring understanding of the Word of GOD into your heart and mind so it becomes a reality within to your whole being. Your spirit will then become quickened to GOD'S Word, and you will begin to think and see like GOD sees and thinks and speak like GOD speaks. You will find yourself pouring over HIS Word -- hungering for more and more. The FATHER rewards those who diligently seek HIM. (Hebrews 11:6.)

Meditate upon the Scriptures listed with these prayers. These are by no means the only Scriptures on these certain subjects, but they are just a beginning as you continue to grow in the LORD; becoming rooted and grounded in HIS Word.

These prayers are to be a help and a guide to you in order for you to become better acquainted with your Heavenly FATHER and HIS Word. Not only does HIS Word affect your life, but also it affects others around you, for you will be able to counsel accurately those who come to you for advice. If you cannot counsel someone with the Word of GOD and HIS Promises; and above all, if you are not being led by the HOLY SPIRIT to share, you should be careful not give to counsel. Walk in GOD'S Counsel, and prize HIS Wisdom. (Psalms 1; Proverbs 4:7-8.) People are looking for something on which they can depend. When someone in need comes to you, you can point them to that portion in GOD'S Word that is the answer to his or her problem and HE then becomes their defense and you are removed from giving incorrect counsel. You become victorious, trustworthy, and known to be the one with the answer, for your heart is fixed and established on HIS Word. (Psalm 112.)

Once you begin delving into GOD'S Word, you must commit to ordering your conversation aright. (Psalms 50:23.) That is being a doer of the Word. HE always has a good report. You cannot pray effectively for yourself, for someone, or about something and then speak negatively about the matter. (Matthew 12:34-37.) This is being double-minded, and being a double minded person will receive *nothing* from GOD. (James 1:6-8.)

In Ephesians 4:29-30 it is written:

***"Let no fault or polluting language, nor evil word, nor unwholesome or worthless talk (ever) come out of your mouth; but only such (speech) as is good and beneficial to the spiritual progress of others, as is fitting to the need and the occasion, that it may be a blessing and give grace (GOD'S favor) to those who hear it. And do not grieve the HOLY SPIRIT of GOD, (do not offend, or vex, or sadden HIM) by whom you were sealed (marked, branded as GOD'S own, secured) for the day of redemption -- of final deliverance through CHRIST from evil and the consequences of sin"*** *(Amplified).*

Allowing of GOD'S Words to sink deep within your innermost being. Our FATHER has much, to say about the tiniest member of the outer body, the tongue, which James speaks as being untamed. (James 3.) Do not give the devil any opportunity by getting into worry, unforgiveness, strife, or criticism. Put a stop to idle and foolish talking. (Ephesians 4:27; 5:4.) You are to be a blessing to others. (Galatians 6:10.)

**Talk the answer, not the problem.** THE ANSWER IS IN GOD'S WORD. You must have knowledge of the Word -- Revelation knowledge. (I Corinthians 2:7-16.)

When strong intercessors are united with one another in prayer, they have the Power of GOD to move mountains. United prayer is a mighty weapon that the body of CHRIST uses. But keep in mind that when you become very familiar with other strong and true intercessors that you share the Word of GOD with; remember total agreement in prayer is what brings the answers according to the Word of GOD.

Believe you received the answer when you pray. Confess the Word. Be bold and declare the Word of GOD over your situations. Hold fast to your confession of faith in GOD'S Word. Allow your spirit, by the HOLY SPIRIT, to pray through you. Praise GOD for the victory now before you even see any manifestation of the answer to those prayers. **Walk by faith and not by sight.** (II Corinthians 5:7.)

Do not be moved by adverse circumstances. As Satan attempts to challenge you, resist him, be steadfast in the faith−letting patients have her perfect work. (James 1:4.) Take the Sword of the Spirit and the Shield of Faith to quench every fiery dart. (Ephesians 6:16.) The entire work of CHRIST on Calvary was for you. Satan has now become a defeated foe, because JESUS conquered him. (Colossians 2:14-15.) We are overcomers by the Blood of the Lamb and the Word of our testimony. (Revelation 12:11.) Fight the good fight of faith. (I Timothy 6:12.) You must stand immovable against the adversary and be firm in faith against his onset; be rooted, establish, strong, and determined. (I Peter 5:9.) Speak GOD'S Word boldly and courageously.

Your desires should be to please and to bless the FATHER. As you pray in line with HIS Word, HE joyfully hears you, as HIS child, and is delighted as we live and walk in the Truth. (III John 4.)

How exciting to know that the prayers of the saints (GOD'S Believers) are forever in the Throne Room. (Revelation 5:8.) Hallelujah!

Praise GOD for HIS Word since HE is the Unlimited GOD when it comes to the fervent prayer of a Righteous Believer, in the Name of JESUS. It belongs to every Child of GOD. Therefore, run with patience the race that is set before you. (Hebrews 12:1-2.) GOD'S Word is able to build you up and give you your rightful inheritance among all GOD'S Children. (Acts 20:32.)

**Commit yourself to pray and to pray correctly by approaching the Throne of GOD with your mouth filled with HIS Word!**

# Introduction

*"The earnest (heart-felt, continued) prayer of a righteous man makes tremendous power available – dynamic in its working"* (James 5:16 Amplified.)

Prayer is fellowshipping with the FATHER – a vital, personal contact with the GOD, Who is more than enough; HE is Jehovah Jireh – our Provider. We are to be in constant communion with HIM *"for the eyes of the LORD are upon the righteous – those who are upright and in right standing with GOD – and HIS ears are attentive (open) to their prayer"* (I Peter 3:12 Amplified).

Prayer is not to be a religious form with no power; it is to be effective, accurate and bursting with powerful results. GOD watches over HIS Word to perform it. (Jeremiah 1:12).

Prayer that brings results must be based with GOD'S Word.

*"For the Word that GOD speaks is alive and full of Power – making it active, operative, energizing and effective; it is sharper than any Two-edged Sword, penetrating to the dividing line of the Breath of Life (soul or mind) and (the immortal) spirit, and of joints and marrow (that is, of the deepest parts of our nature) exposing and sifting and analyzing and judging the very thoughts and purposes of the heart"* (Hebrews 4:12 Amplified).

Prayer is the "**living**" Word within our mouths. Our mouths must speak forth the Word of Faith, for work of faith is what pleases GOD. (Hebrews 11:6.) We hold HIS Word up to HIM in prayer, and our FATHER sees HIMSELF working within HIS Word.

GOD'S Word is our contact with HIM. We put HIM in remembrance of HIS Word (Isaiah 43:26) placing a demand on HIS Resource and ability, in the Name of our LORD JESUS. We remind HIM that HE supplies all of our needs according to HIS riches in Glory by CHRIST JESUS. (Philippians 4:19.) HIS Word does not return to HIM void, – therefore, without producing any effect, it is useless; but it *will* accomplish that which HE pleases and purposes, and it will prosper in the things for which HE sent it. (Isaiah 55:11.) Hallelujah! (*Hallelujah* is interpreted as the *Highest Word of Thanks*." It is also the only individual word throughout the world that is understood, in all the languages of this world, "**Hallelujah**" is always understood, there is no other word that could ever replace the word for HALLELUJAH! (*Amen*, is interpreted as: *So be it, or it is DONE*.)

GOD did not leave us without HIS thoughts and HIS ways for we have HIS Word – HIS bond through the Blood of JESUS CHRIST. GOD instructs us to call upon HIM and HE will answer and show us great and mighty things. (Jeremiah 33:3.) Prayer is to be exciting – not a drudging act. In fact, having an ongoing Relationship GOD continually grows stronger and stronger, increasing our faith with such a boldness and courage that rises up against any obstacle.

It takes someone to pray, which moves GOD especially when we pray with an earnest fervent faith; for GOD always knows what is within the heart of any person and HE considers one who works their heart of faith–as Righteousness. HE says that HIS Eyes run to and from throughout the whole earth to show HIMSELF strong in behalf of those whose heart is blameless toward HIM (that is covered with the Blood of JESUS). (Ephesians 1:4).) We are HIS very own children. (Ephesians 1:5.) We are HIS Righteousness in CHRIST JESUS. (II Corinthians 5:21.) HE tells us to come boldly before the Throne of Grace, to *obtain* HIS Mercy and to find Grace to help in the time of need – appropriate and well-timed help. (Hebrews 4:16.) GOD'S timing is always perfect, **"HE is always an on time GOD."**

The request to the FATHER asking to be given the Full of Armor of GOD is for every believer, every member of the body of CHRIST, who are willing to put on the Full Armor of GOD and learn to walk in it, is prepared every spiritual weapon for any spiritual warfare, which are *not carnal* but Mighty through GOD for the pulling down of the strongholds of the enemy (Satan, the prince of this world, and all his demonic forces). Spiritual warfare will often take place especially in intercession prayer. (II Corinthians 10:4, Ephesians 6:12.)

There are many different kinds of prayer, such as the prayer of thanksgiving and praise, the prayer of dedication and worship, and the prayers that bring phenomenal changes of *things* in this world, but GOD will never change, **"HE is the same, yesterday, today, and forever."** All prayer involves our time of fellowshipping with the GOD, the FATHER.

In Ephesians 6, we are instructed to take the Sword of the Spirit which is the Word of GOD.

*(Ephesians 6:18 Amplified)* **"...pray at all times – on every occasion, in every season – in the Spirit, with all manner (different kinds) of prayer and entreaty".**

In I Timothy 2 we are admonished and urged that **prayer is our responsibility.**

*(I Timothy 2:1 Amplified)* **"...petitions, prayers, intercessions and thanksgiving be offered on behalf of all men."**

Prayer must be the foundation for every Believing Christian endeavor. Prayer of a Righteous fervent person never fails. We are **not** to be ignorant concerning GOD'S Word and we should desire to really know HIS Word and Promises so we don't pray amiss. GOD desires for HIS people to be successful, to be filled with HIS fullness that is deep, and having a clear understanding and knowledge of HIS Perfect Will (HIS Word), and to bear fruit in every good work. (Colossians 1:9-13.) We then bring honor and Glory to HIM. (John 15:8.) HE desires that we know how to pray effectively as HE admonishes us in Proverbs and in James 5: 16 which is the key verse of the Book.

*(James 5:16)* **"The effective fervent prayer of a righteous man avails much."**

*(Proverbs 15:8)* **"...the prayer of the upright is HIS delight."**

Our FATHER has not left us helpless. Not only has HE given us HIS Word, but HE also has given us the HOLY SPIRIT to help in our infirmities when we do not know how to pray correctly for different situations. (Romans 8:26.) Praise GOD! Our FATHER has provided HIS people with every possible avenue to insure their complete and total victory in this life to come forth, in the Name of our LORD JESUS CHRIST. (I John 5:3-5.)

**We pray to the FATHER, in the Name of JESUS, through the HOLY SPIRIT, according to GOD'S Word!**

Using GOD'S Word, specifically in prayer, is the main purpose of prayer, and it is a most effective and accurate means. JESUS said:

*(John 6:63 Amplified)* ***"The Words (of Truth) that I have been speaking to you are Spirit and Life."***

When JESUS faced Satan in the wilderness, HE said again and again, **"...it is written...it is written...it is written."** We are to live, be upheld, and sustained by every Word that proceeds from the Mouth of GOD. (Matthew 4:4.)

James, by the Spirit, admonishes that when we do not have answers to prayer it is because have not asked; or we ask and receive not because we ask amiss (not according to HIS Word or according to HIS Perfect Will, for HIS Word is HIS Perfect Will). (James 4:2-3.) It is imperative as an Intercessor, and even as a Christian, that we allow the Word of GOD to admonish us to become experts in using the Power of Prayer, rightly dividing the Word of Truth. (II Timothy 2:15.)

Using the Word in prayer is **not** taking it out of context, for HIS Word in us is the key to answered prayer – prayer that brings results. HE is always able to do exceedingly abundantly above all that we could ask or think, according to the Power that works in us. (Ephesians 3:20.) Take notice that it says, ***"according to the power that works in us,"*** remember the whole concept of faith is the concept of one who has learned how to work their faith according to the Word of GOD, which is what we will be judged by on that great Judgment Day. Too many Christians or believers lack the understanding or the definition of the term "**FAITH**." Faith believes for something that is not presently seen. Therefore, faith is an act through prayer of asking for something (according to the Word) ONE TIME and then leaving it in GOD'S Hands. Your follow-up will be our responsibility to daily come before GOD with thanksgiving to the FATHER for the answer of that prayer. Prayer is like an investment, as you pray in the Spirit, as the HOLY SPIRIT instructs you; you will want to find the results of your investment to see the answers of GOD'S Faithfulness to HIS Word, to see that your effective prayers are coming into being. Too many times, the mortal part of us, wants to take what we had asked for, out of the Hand of GOD and we many times make the mistake of trying to attempt to resolve the problem or feel that we need or should be doing something in order for the answer to come. The only time we take any steps to be a vessel to resolve the problem is ONLY when we are prompted by the HOLY SPIRIT. The Power of prayer which is within GOD'S Word. It is anointed by the HOLY SPIRIT. The Spirit of GOD does not lead us apart from the Word, for the Word is from the Spirit is GOD, Who is the

Resource to all of our requests. When we learn to apply HIS Word personally within ourselves and to others–not adding or taking from it– in the Name of JESUS, is when we will see the results. We apply the Word to the **now situation**, and to those things, circumstances, and situations facing each of us at the very moment in time.

Paul was very specific and definite in his praying. The first Chapters of Ephesians, Philippians, Colossians, and II Thessalonians are examples of how Paul prayed for believers. There are numerous others that you should search out in your own time as you study and meditate within HIS Word. Paul wrote under the inspiration of the HOLY SPIRIT. We can and should be using these Spirit-given prayers on a daily basis! That is why this book will conclude with examples of how to pray as an intercessor. At the beginning you will probably use these examples to pray, but DO NOT allow them to become prayers of repetition. Each believer who desires to see GOD moving in their lives should learn how to pray according to the Word of GOD; again these illustrated prayers, are to teach us how we should learn how to become an effective pray warrior through the leading of the HOLY SPIRIT. A good example of this, which I will elaborate in a later chapter, but it basically deals with the time when the disciples ask JESUS to teach them to pray. JESUS answered them with a prayer of example, a simple model prayer, that was **not** meant to be prayed repetitiously, but with understanding of what and how HE was teaching them to pray:

*(Matthew 6:5-13)* **"And when you pray, you should not be like the hypocrites. For they love to pray standing in the synagogues and on the corners of the streets, that they may be seen by men. Assuredly, I say to you, they have their reward.**

*(6) But you, when you pray, go into your room, and when you have shut your door, pray to your FATHER who is in the secret place; and your FATHER who sees in secret will reward you openly.*

*(7) And when you pray, do not use vain repetitions as the heathen do. For they think that they will be heard for their many words.*

*(8) Therefore do not be like them. For your FATHER knows the things you have need of before you ask HIM.*

*(9) In this manner, therefore, pray (or, this is an example of how to learn to pray):*

*"Our FATHER in Heaven, Hallowed (Holy) is YOUR Name.*

*(10) Your Kingdom come. YOUR (Word) will be done on earth as it is in Heaven.*

*(11) Give us this day our daily bread.*

*(12) And forgive us our debts, as we forgive our debtors (Prayer for forgiveness is qualified by a readiness to forgive personal injury, those who have hurt us in any way; verses 14-15 say, For if you forgive men their trespasses, your Heavenly FATHER will also forgive you. But if you do not forgive men their trespasses, neither will Your FATHER forgive your trespasses.)*

*(13) And do not lead us into temptation (please keep in mind that GOD will never tempt us, but HE will allow the enemy to tempt or test our faith), but GOD will always be in our presence to deliver us from the*

*evil one. For YOURS is the Kingdom and the Power and the Glory Forever. Amen (or, let it be so).*

Verse 13 is extremely important in our work of faith, since it is the final petition when you are requesting GOD to strengthen you to withstand immoral peril, in case the petitioner fails in his work of faith and becomes overwhelmed by the temptation of the **evil one**.

In II Corinthians 1:11, II Corinthians 9:14, and Philippians 1:4, we see examples of how believers prayed for one another – putting others first in their prayer life with *"the spirit of joy."* Our faith works by the Power of GOD'S Perfect Love. (Galatians 5:6.) For the Scriptures also tells us when we call forth GOD'S Perfect Love to be poured upon someone who has hurt us in any way and most important of all, is after we have forgiven them, GOD's Perfect Love is like heaping coals of fire upon their heads. We grow spiritually as we reach out to help others– praying for and by holding them up to GOD or turning them over to GOD for HIM to resolve any issue, for HIS Ways Right and full of Perfect Justice according to the Word of Life. (Philippians 2:16.)

Man is a spirit, he has a soul, and he lives in a body. (I Thessalonians 5:23.) In order to operate successfully, each of these three parts must be spiritually fed properly. The soul or intellect needs to be fed with spiritual food to produce GOD'S Powerful and spiritual strength. The spirit, the heart or the inward man, is the real you, the part that has been reborn in CHRIST JESUS. It also must be fed initially with the Milk of the Word and as we grow we begin to desire and hunger for wholesome spiritual food which is GOD'S Word in order to produce and develop one's faith that is rooted and grounded in the Word. As we feast upon GOD'S Word, our minds become renewed by HIS Word, and we have a fresh mental and spiritual attitude. (Ephesians 4:23-24.)

There was a moment when the disciples tried to cast out a demon and were unsuccessful. But JESUS quickly told them that this happens through prayer and fasting. Now in today's world we have a totally wrong concept of "**fasting**," we usually think is just not eating, but true fasting is when you are missing meals you are spending time within GOD'S Word and HIS Word is becoming your spiritual food. For example, from my own life; **when I have had spiritual fasts and would spend time devouring the Word of GOD as my spiritual food, the neat result was that I "*never*" lost one pound.** But if I decided to have a regular fast, by not eating physical food, then I lose weight. This is so important to understand as the Ways of GOD in learning HIS Principle and Standards.

Likewise, we are to present our bodies as a living sacrifice, holy, acceptable unto GOD (Romans 12:1) and not allow our body or its desires to dominate us, but to bring it into subjection to the spiritual being. (I Corinthians 9:27.) GOD'S Word is healing and health to all our flesh. (Proverbs 4:22.) Therefore, GOD'S Word affects each part of us–spirit, soul (mind), and body. We become virtually united to the FATHER, through JESUS and the HOLY SPIRIT – becoming one with Them. (John 16:13-15, John 17:21, Colossians 2:10.)

GOD'S Word, this spirit food, takes root in our hearts and minds; and when we allow it to come forth from our mouth we are in the process of taming or taking control of our physical tongue to speak words that are pure, edifying and righteous, and when we speak forth GOD'S Word from our mouth, it will produce much. This is GOD'S creative working power. The unspoken Word works only as we are bold to confess it and then respond in obedience to the Word of GOD.

Be doers of the Word, and not hearers only, deceiving your own selves. (James 1:22.) Faith without works or corresponding actions is "*dead*." (James 2:17.) Do not be mental assenters (*the expression of approval or agreement*–Oxford Dictionary)–those who agree that the Word of GOD is true, but never act on it will miss out on GOD'S blessings. **Real faith is responding to GOD'S Word in the "NOW."** We cannot build faith without practicing or proving HIS Word. True, initially everyone has been given the same measure of faith, but as you hold fast to the Word, as you learn more from the Word and live by the Word–your faith grows and becomes stronger as you mature by feeding on the Word of GOD. We cannot develop an effective prayer life that does not consist to be built upon the foundation of GOD'S Word or they are empty words. It is not until GOD'S Word actually is a total part of our prayer life that we can see it working in a mighty way. We are to hold fast to our "*confession*" by the Truth of GOD'S Word. Our LORD JESUS is the High Priest of our confession (Hebrews 3:1), and HE is the Guarantee of a better agreement–a more excellent and advantageous covenant or fulfillment of GOD'S Promises. (Hebrews 7:22.)

**Prayer does not cause faith to work, but steadfast and firm faith that comes in line with the Word of GOD is what causes prayer to work.** Therefore, any prayer problem is a problem of the having a spirit of doubt–doubting the integrity of the Word and of the ability of

GOD to stand behind HIS Promises or the statements of fact in HIS Word.

We can spend fruitless hours of prayer, if our hearts are not prepared beforehand, then we will not reap the fruit of our prayers. The preparation of the heart, the spirit, comes from meditation in the GOD'S Word, meditation within the Word teaches or reveal to us who we are in CHRIST, and Who HE is to us and what the HOLY SPIRIT can do within us as we become GOD-inside minded. As GOD told Joshua (Joshua 1:8), we meditate on the Word day and night, do according to all that is written, and then our way will be made prosperous and have good success. We are to attend to GOD'S Word, submit to HIS sayings, keep them in the center of our hearts, and put away contrary talk. (Proverbs 4:20-24.) Regarding meditation: this is the reason why Intercessors become alerted, wide awake, in the middle of the night, why, because our minds are not occupied with the busyness of our daily life. In psychology there are two mind sets, the alpha, and the beta. The alpha is when you are alert and busy, in the routine of life; therefore, your mediation level is not at its best until you learn to be extremely become aware to the leading of the HOLY SPIRIT; while in the beta state of mind, is a mind of meditation, it is quieted and still so you can hear the Voice of the LORD and the HOLY SPIRIT. That is why the HOLY SPIRIT will alert you or waken you in the middle of the night since you are more apt to listen to HIM. If you remember the story about Samuel, GOD always called to him in the middle of the night, saying, "*Samuel*" and he would think that it was Eli calling him. Samuel would run to Eli and say, "*Here am I, what do you want?*" By the fourth time of this same event, Eli told

Samuel to say to GOD, "***Speak, LORD, for your servant hears.***" (I Samuel 3:10.)

When we use GOD'S Word in prayer, this is ***not*** something we just rush through praying once, and we are finished. Do ***not*** be mistaken. There is nothing "magical" nor "manipulative" about it – no set pattern or device in order to satisfy what we want or think out of our flesh. Instead we are holding GOD'S Word before HIM, knowing according to HIS Word that it will never return to HIM void or without a return for our good. We confess what HE says belongs to us. To many Christians may think prayer is this great magical act and then quickly become discouraged when the answers do not come within their lives. Answers to prayer come by FAITH, and FAITH is work as you speak forth GOD'S Word!

***"We expect HIS divine intervention while we choose not to look at the things that are seen, but the things that are unseen, for the things that are seen are subject to change."*** (II Corinthians 4:18.)

Prayer based upon the Word that rises above our senses, it contacts the Author of the Word and sets HIS Spiritual Laws into motion. It is not just saying prayers bring forth the results, but it is spending time with the FATHER, learning HIS wisdom, HIS Ways, HIS Principle and Standards that draw us into the Power of HIS Strength, being filled with HIS Quietness, and basking in HIS Love is what brings results to our prayers. Praise the LORD!

# Learning How to Become an Effective Intercessor

"Number one, being a worshipper is essential, since it is the pathway to come before the Throne of GOD. Bath yourself in the songs taken from the Psalms or the different Scriptures in the Word of GOD; allow them to be burnt or to be sealed within your heart. The Word put to music is one of the best ways to allow the Word of GOD to penetrate deep within the heart and the mind. I am sure that you have heard different people sing or hum just a portion of a song and it then begin to go through you mind; especially to a person who is a musician that tune will continually go over and over with the mind until you complete the song. That is how the Word to music works responds to one and as the words go over and over within mind and heart you begin to allow it to grow deep within the heart.

Allow yourself to truly know the HOLY SPIRIT and HIS Voice. Initially, you will utilize the intercessor prayers within this book, but the more familiar you become with the Word of GOD or the Promises of GOD'S Word; the Gifts of the HOLY SPIRIT will also become familiar within your life and you will be able to discern even the different spirits in this world; that is when you will become an effective Intercessor or Prayer Warrior for the Glory of GOD. Pray in the Spirit, when only a name comes to your mind. Since GOD already knows the person probably better than the person knows them self, their problem or situation is thoroughly known by GOD, Who holds the solution in HIS Hand. But HE needs you to be the confessor of HIS Word in order to bind the enemy, for when we bind the enemy here on earth, we then are loosening the Power of GOD in Heaven to work here on earth and bring forth the answers to our requests.

You will find that during intercession you will be led to bind and loose, or even if led by the HOLY SPIRIT to find another trustworthy intercessor who you are confident is trustworthy to share part of the situation so you can come into an agreement in prayer according to Matthew 18:18-19 *"(18) Assuredly, I say to you, whatever you <u>bind on earth</u> will be <u>bound in heaven</u>, and whatever you <u>loose on earth</u> will be <u>loosed in heaven</u>. (19) Again, I say to you that if two of you agree on earth concerning anything that they ask, it will be done for them by My FATHER in Heaven."* The important fact about GOD'S concept of binding and losing those things in prayer is because prayer is a form of battle and we are spiritual warriors against the enemy. Therefore, whatever you bind on earth, it becomes empty, and that is the moment when you loosen GOD'S Promises or resolution so it will immediately filled the void, or the enemy is quick to fill any form of emptiness to thwart your desire in prayer. The same concept goes with loosing anything on earth, you must be quick with the Word of GOD to fill it with GOD'S Promises.

Intercession will **first** begin through worship (that is why I love to sing in the Spirit, it is an excellent way to prepare your heart, mind or soul to come before the Throne of GOD); **secondly**, acknowledge the GOD Head, the FATHER, SON and HOLY SPIRIT, HIS Omnipotence (power), HIS Omnipresence (forever presence) and HIS Omniscience (HIS ability to knows all things). **Thirdly**, make sure you are in right standing with the FATHER that you stand completely under the Blood of CHRIST JESUS. Allow the HOLY SPIRIT to search your heart regarding any unforgiveness and make sure that all things are upright before GOD within your heart. **Fourthly**, is binding or taking authority over the enemy, in JESUS Name (you will learn real quick, as an Intercessor or a Prayer Warrior, that the enemy will get to know who you are and will probably attempt to thwart your own life without having any success, because GOD has made you to become mindful of his deceitful ways). Remember the demonic person who said to the believers, "*JESUS I know, and Paul I know; but who are you?*" (Acts 19:15), this is the Power of having a Spiritual Fast. Why? Because JESUS and Paul were true intercessors and Satan know the Power they had through GOD. When dealing with the enemy and his cohorts, make sure you DO NOT walk out from under the "*umbrella*" of the Blood of JESUS; I often use the term, "*stepping out from under the umbrella.*" **Fifthly**, come before the FATHER, in JESUS' Name, with your request; if led by the SPIRIT only use the name of the individual, if you know the problem, bind their situation, and confess HIS Word calling forth GOD'S Promises to bring forth the answer. **Last of all**; spend time in thanksgiving and praising GOD in the Spirit as in the First step.

Follow-up: is always important as you invest your time in prayer as an Intercessor, for it is similar as an investment of money in a bank; don't you want to know the results of your time of investment in intercession? If you have just started with intercession; the answer is not finished until your act of faith goes from nothing until you receive the answer. Therefore, until you receive your investment or answer, continue to follow the above steps: (1), (2), (3), (4), the fifth step becomes slightly different; announce to the FATHER the name or situation of the individual and confess the answer with GOD'S Promises. Trust me, the HOLY SPIRIT will show you how to pray effectively. But most important of all, this last step is to take time to give thanksgiving until it is **DONE or completed!**

As I have shared, the most important part of being an effective Intercessor is to learn how to pray according to the Word of GOD and HIS Promises with a heart of thanksgiving for the answer. But it is just as important to walk in the Wisdom, Knowledge and Understanding of GOD Ways regarding problems, sicknesses, and different circumstances within each individual's life. Therefore, it is important to learn as much as possible, especially regarding sicknesses or illnesses so that we do not pray amiss.

The more knowledge you acquire regarding the numerous types of illnesses, the more effective you can be as an Intercessor to battle the enemy. Always keep in mind that our GOD is Omniscient, and HE is faithful to disclose or reveal HIS Knowledge and Wisdom even in the area of scientific and in the medical field. Be diligent to ask thorough questions from physicians, professionals or educated individuals, especially regarding different types of illnesses, psychological situations such as depression and being knowledgeable regarding finances; so you know how to pray effectively. The majority of times these educated individuals will give you answers that may sometimes appear to be discouraging or sound negative or even pessimistic; but as an Intercessor that information is very valuable and it is up to you to turn the negative into a positive through the Power of the Promises of GOD'S Word. Also, never be fearful of bad news, for GOD has a master plan for every situation to turn bad situations for our good.

Now, as an Intercessor, is when your work begins. Research the Word of GOD, this is why it is very important as an Intercessor to know the Word of GOD, to know how to search the Scriptures to find the Powerful Promises to thwart and hinder the works of the enemy.

A perfect example of researching any form of illness, such as the different types of cancer, is to realize that no matter how excellent GOD has created us as human beings; always be aware or enlightened that Satan, his demons, his cohorts, his fallen angels are continually in the midst of this world. Satan's job, as well as all of his team members, are to destroy or tear down both believers in JESUS CHRIST and unbelievers. After GOD created Adam and Eve, he commissioned them to begin to procreate this world. Scientifically, we are very much aware that life begins with a single cell.

It doesn't matter if you believe in the literal six days of creation or if it took a span of time for in HIS Word it shares that to GOD, "*A thousand years is like one day and one day is like a thousand years.*" (II Peter 3:8). So why should we be taken in or have unjustified disagreements with such theological terminology. As I have been studying and mediating in the Word of GOD, I am seeing more and more of GOD'S scientific methods in HIS Ways. Plus if GOD felt it was important for us to know all things, HE would have put it within HIS Word; then what or how useful would the works of our faith be?

Cancer also begins as a mutated cell−which shows the work of Satan's evil powers. It is sad to say, but true, it is Satan's work to take those mutated cells and through his powers which he allows them to devour the good cells, but knowing that GOD is our Creator, why should we fret or become anxious because GOD is the one Who is behind the discovery of all of the different types of medications. As believers we will often question these works with, "**Why**?" We can even become a doubting Thomas; when we often cop out by misquoting or abusing the Word of GOD. We may often say, "If GOD be for us, who can be against us, but not truly believe it to its fullness." Many times we forget that it is GOD'S Will is that we learn to go through the flood and the fire which is the only way that that causes us to realize in order for our faith to grow. Too often, we want to blame GOD for the different negative circumstances in our lives, but without those circumstances how would our faith ever grow and become strong; and I should make it clear that GOD can and will "**never**" bring forth negative things within our lives, since HE only knows how to bring forth good things that are the best for us. Therefore, how will we ever learn to become confident that we serve an awesome GOD, whose Grace is sufficient in every situation.

How will we ever know that we serve a Mighty GOD, Who can do the impossible, Who can move mountains and Who can strengthen your faith so you can proclaim that you serve a miracle working GOD.

Look at the prophet Daniel, who was steadfast in the Word of GOD; who was confident that his GOD would not fail him. What did he do? He declared the Word of the LORD and GOD'S Angels to be encamped about him, and the GOD'S Angels either shut the mouths of every lion or filled their tummies to the point that they were not hungry (not scriptural; but we do know the Scriptures do tell us when the prison guards who went in to the den to remove Daniel from the den of lions, they were devoured by the lions).

Throughout GOD'S Scriptures we can see again and again where GOD allowed Satan to challenge HIS children. Again, "**Why**?" Because GOD wanted us to put our trust in HIM to give us the concept of how to use our faith; in turn, GOD proved that Satan was and still is deceitful in his ways, as GOD'S children use their faith and trust in Almighty GOD; the greatest reward was when GOD declared, *"your faith has made you Righteous."* (Romans 4:5).

Are we foolish children? Are we foolish enough to think that life is a bed of roses? Remember every beautiful rose which grows on a stem, each stem has many thorns. This is a perfect example of life in this world. It is the next world, the New Heaven and New Earth where Satan is a defeated foe; no sickness, no pain, no calamity, no grief, etc. Then why are we in this world? According to the simple Gospel, since GOD has given us our own will, it is our time, or opportunity to make an important decision to make JESUS CHRIST to be LORD of our life or to deny HIM as LORD. That is the choice GOD has given to every individual when HE gave us our own will to make our own decisions. But the most important decision each individual has to make in this life is to choose who they want to serve as their own master and lord; will it be GOD or the enemy?

*(**The example prayers are written in masculine gender; please change the gender respectfully:** him/she, his/her, etc. *Also, keep in mind that if you are using multiple individuals, change the written possessive form to* **their** *or* **them**.)*

# The Powerful Example of The LORD'S Prayer

A good example that JESUS shared is *"The LORD'S Prayer"* but keep in mind, HE made it very clear not to be as the hypocrite (by putting on a show or to pray with in a vain concept) and not to be repetitious, that why it is important to really fill your heart and mind with GOD'S Promises within HIS Word so our prayers will become extremely effective and directly from our spiritual heart that comes in line with GOD'S Word.

Take notice to the different parts of The LORD'S Prayer:

*(9) In this manner, therefore, pray (or, this is an example of how to learn to pray):*

*"Our FATHER in Heaven, Hallowed (Holy) is YOUR Name.*

*(10) Your Kingdom [will] come. YOUR (Word) will be done on earth as it is in Heaven. (11) Give us this day our daily bread (meet our every daily need).*

*(12) And forgive us our debts, as we forgive our debtors (Prayer for forgiveness is qualified by a readiness to forgive personal injury; verses 14-15 say, 'For if you forgive men their trespasses, your Heavenly FATHER will also forgive you.'* "*But if you do not forgive men their trespasses, neither will your FATHER forgive your trespasses."*

***(13) And do not (allow the enemy) to lead us into temptation, but deliver us from the evil one. For YOURS is the Kingdom and the Power and the Glory Forever. Amen** (or, let it be so).*

Verse 13 is extremely important in the working of your faith or the works of faith, since it is the final petition when you are requesting GOD to strengthen you to stand with immoral peril, in case the petitioner fails in his work of faith and becomes overwhelmed by the temptation of the **evil one**.

Let's allow the LORD'S model prayer to become a strong part of our life and as we pray this prayer in churches or wherever we are, don't allow the repetition of the prayer loose its Powerful message of how to pray effectively.

We first are acknowledging the FATHER'S location and HIS Holiness. The Word of GOD says, whatever is bound on earth is also bound in Heaven, but it is up to us to loose GOD'S Word in Heaven in order for it to loosen for the situation here on earth.

Secondly, we are acknowledging (this is extremely a comforting fact) this is GOD'S Kingdom, not Satan's kingdom; Satan has already been defeated at Calvary, through the Blood, the Death and the Resurrection of JESUS CHRIST. Also, keep in mind that JESUS now sits at the Right Hand of the FATHER, as the GREAT INTERCESSOR! HALLELUJAH!

Thirdly, "*give us our daily bread*"; this is our time of requesting and confessing by faith the Promises of GOD'S Word.

Fourthly, we want to make sure that nothing in our life is causing us to be outside of the umbrella in this world's rain. Which is why most times unanswered prayer comes from people or intercessors who may have some unforgiven situation that is hindering their prayer life, which is not under the Blood of JESUS. You cannot come to the FATHER but through JESUS' atonement on the Cross. Again, the HOLY SPIRIT will show you where you stand, HE will convince you if there is anything within your heart and life that needs to be put under the Blood of JESUS. Years ago we would often use the word "convict," I personally don't like that word, it sounds negative and my GOD is so far from being negative. I believe the HOLY SPIRIT **"convinces us"** (according to the Greek definition of the word convict) of our wrongs so we have a better understanding to immediately release those burdens to be made right before GOD. We are still human beings, what makes us different is that we stand under the Blood of CHRIST, Righteous and made Holy before the FATHER, so HE will hear our petitions and answer them.

Again, verse 13 is extremely important in the work of faith, since it is the final petition when you are requesting GOD, which is to strengthen you as an immoral being, who is not apt to fall short of the Glory of GOD in their work of faith and being overwhelmed by the temptation of the **evil one**.

Last of all, is acknowledging GOD'S awesome Power! ***"YOURS is the Kingdom and the Power and the Glory Forever. Amen (or, let it be so)."*** HE is Omnipotent and HIS Glory or anointing fills HIS Throne.

Again, what I shared before: Sometimes Intercessors become too excited and they think if they can lay hands on a person that the anointing will always flow into another being. That is not always true, in fact, most times it can become a hindrance, always wait for the HOLY SPIRIT to give you discernment or the okay, as HE instructs you. You should never lay hands on a person until the HOLY SPIRIT instructs you to do so. Why? If a person is not ready to receive what GOD has for them, your act of faith is ineffective.

# The Apostles Creed

A particular proclamation we do repeat as a confession of our basic doctrine is the Apostles Creed, since it declares the major universal doctrine of Christianity. This is a good concept when speaking with people from different denominations as far as what they believe; it is not to judge them, but to be aware and careful in order to be sensitive to the HOLY SPIRIT while you are in conversation.

*I believe in GOD the FATHER Almighty,*

*Maker of Heaven and earth:*

*And in JESUS CHRIST, HIS only SON and our LORD,*

*Who was conceived by the HOLY SPIRIT,*

*Born of the Virgin Mary,*

*Suffered under Pontius Pilate,*

*Was crucified, dead, and buried:*

*HE descended into hell;*

*The third day HE rose again from the dead;*

*HE ascended into Heaven,*

*And sits at the Right Hand of GOD the FATHER Almighty;*

*From there HE will come to judge the quick and the dead.*

*I believe in the HOLY SPIRIT;*

*The Christian Church; the communion of saints (Believers);*

*The Forgiveness of sins; the Resurrection of the Church of CHRIST,*

*And the Life Everlasting. Amen.*

(Music has been composed as a song to be sung after proclaiming our doctrines, which we believe and hold onto steadfastly.)

# What about Intercession for the Unbeliever?

As Intercessors, we should treat all humanity as a brother or sister. Who are we to judge a person, only GOD knows the hearts of every individual? We have too many Christians walking around, attending church, thinking they are holier than thou; these people scare me, according to the Scriptures they are walking down an unsafe road. When it comes to sin, we should be more concerned about ourselves instead of everyone else. In Titus 3:1-5, the Apostle Paul reminds us of proper conduct toward the outside world; a remembrance of our own worldly behavior prior our pre-converted lives and now having the realization of the Love, Mercy, Grace and Kindness that GOD has towards us. Paul also wrote in his letters giving list of sins, they were never for the unbeliever, but for the believers themselves; especially since Paul recognized that he was truly a sinner saved by GOD'S Grace.

But what is more important is that you, as an intercessor, you are meek and mild, yet one who walks in GOD'S Authority and Power; in other words, you are not to be a push over. Know the true meanings of GOD'S Grace, Mercy, Peace and Love. Yet remember how JESUS entered into the Temple was turned over the tables and it appeared to many that HE was bringing havoc to their good deeds, when in reality, JESUS saw them as hypocrites using the Temple as a market place instead of acknowledging as it being the Presence of GOD. Also, remember how JESUS mingled with the sinners, but as HE looked who had a desire to serve HIM after their lives were changed. The definition of Christian is to be like CHRIST JESUS our LORD. As an intercessor, we need to continually walk in humility and love everyone, not being concerned with what religion they are. We should be praying for the Muslims, Hindus, Atheist, etc., especially any and all Fundamental or Liturgical Religions, Denominations and/or Non-denominations.

Most wars start over religious matters. If CHRIST were presently here, I believe HE would be rebuking those who lack HIS Love for all people, including many Christian Denominations. We need to get back to the place of allowing the HOLY SPIRIT to do the convincing of sin within our own hearts and the hearts of others. Many people and Religious leaders are walking down lives' road when they have judgmental spirit towards people who may not be in agreement with them; but it is the obligation to pray for all people that the HOLY SPIRIT will speak to their inner beings and convince them of GOD'S Ways, therefore we should be loving, praying and calling forth unbelievers to come to know JESUS as their LORD and SAVIOR.

We need Intercessors for ministries; Satan has had his foot in the church doors for much too long. I believe through prayer and supplication this can be broken in these last days.

# Worship and its Importance in Preparing You to Receive the Word of GOD

Worship is an extreme important part in the preparation of receiving the Word of GOD whether in a Church service, or at home or whenever the HOLY SPIRIT is bringing to our remembrance GOD'S Word.

These are very similar to the steps within "**The LORD'S Prayer**"; the same is with worship. Years ago and even today in the majority of church services begin with 3 hymns, prayer, offering, maybe a few special songs by individual(s) and/or a choir, it concludes with the Pastor giving a sermon. As we look in the Old Testament (O.T.), especially in the books of Numbers and the Psalms; besides the Levites (the Priests, the first born of every tribe), the tribe of Judah was the first of all the tribes to respond to GOD'S instruction to worship GOD; in fact, the tribe of Judah were always the first to go before the warriors, as they would be praising and worshipping GOD; they were the first responders in any battle, for they knew the battle was always the LORDS.

As we have been taught and as it also is revealed in the Scriptures of the twelve tribes of Israel; one of the major tribes was the tribe of Judah, who were called to be worshippers.

After Moses led the exodus from Egypt and during their time in the wilderness, the twelve tribes of Israel were to set up their tents on all four sides of the tabernacle. On the **East side** (where the sun rose) were the tribes of: **Judah**, Issachar, and Zebulun; on the **West side** (where the sun set) were the tribes of: Ephraim, Manasseh and Benjamin; the **North side** were the tribes of: Dan, Asher, Naptali; and on the **South side** were the tribes of: Reuben, Simeon, and Gad. Counting just the men, all tribes totaled: 603,550 men. Besides the Priest who were set a part to follow the liturgy and sacrifices as instructed by the LORD. The Tribe of Judah was the next level of being the most important tribe. They led the worship preparing the other tribes of Israel in order to prepare the children of Israel for the services performed by the priest in the tabernacle where the HOLY of HOLIES abode. The tribe of Judah's praise brought encouragement to the faith of the children of Israel and as always, they were the first to go into battle. Are you beginning to see the importance of worship? You cannot afford to go into spiritual battle without having praise and worship flowing from your heart and mind in order to become conquerors. Praise and Worship was always the first step of every order from GOD; for there is mighty power through Praise, it strengthens the warring angels to fight in the unseen spiritual battles of the eyes of humans.

I feel today, the Church is missing so much of what GOD has for them because they lack WORSHIP! and I mean true deep and intense worship. It is imperative that Pastors are extremely sensitive to the leading of the HOLY SPIRIT. Pastors are just to be overseers of the people that GOD has entrusted to give them to teach the Full Gospel of JESUS CHRIST. Too many Pastors have taken GOD'S matters into their own hands, which is very scary, because they stand accountable before Almighty GOD in doing so.

I can share from my own experience of growing up in churches that were once a very vibrant experience of seeing the Power of GOD working before their very eyes; being full of Praise and Worship which prepared people to be hearers and doers of the Word as they saw miracles and healing performed by Almighty GOD. This is one thing I do know is lacking within churches today, there is very little worship; you seldom hear people declare a shout of "**Amen**," "**Hallelujah**" or "**Praise GOD**," as a form of agreement of what was being preached from the pulpit. Today's different denominations have only a few vibrant church services where the Power of GOD is still being demonstrated according to GOD'S Word. We are at the point where we need to acknowledge the simplicity of being SPIRIT led, instead of doing what man sets as a form of worship. Years ago, as a young person, I attended two different denominations. I saw the freeness of moving of the HOLY SPIRIT, but as I grew older I began to see a change take place where it slowly began to change and the HOLY SPIRIT seemed to no longer be control as leading the worship services, where it now has become plain and ridged. Even the people are now becoming disgruntled when the service is not over by noon. They have tied the Hands of GOD from allowing the freedom to be true Worshippers as HE has called us to be. You now know what is going to happen next because they were the same steps that would take place every week. There was no more freeness of the SPIRIT. It was imperative to have Sunday morning worship service or the Mass in Catholic Churches; and many of the Sunday evening services were cancelled, and also many of the mid-week Bible Studies have stopped. It is no wonder why the people are lacking faith and the Knowledge of GOD'S Word, for the lack of being hearers of the Word of GOD.

My heart hungers for the old time services where the HOLY SPIRIT was instrumental in moving HIS Power within the churches; I remember the times when I began to search one church after another to found a church that was full of the HOLY SPIRIT, but they were mostly non-denominational churches that had a great moving of the HOLY SPIRIT and when you left the church service, you were filled with excitement, enthusiasm and with a new outlook about yourself, the HOLY SPIRIT was always showing us where changes needed to be made so we could grow closer to the LORD. After moving into a large city and initially I was taken back with the change of the order of many different agendas of these church services. The first was: why is there only one Sunday service on a Sunday, instead of having both a morning and evening service. Also, the lack of having a mid-week service for Bible Study and Prayer services; Churches that want GOD to move in their midst should be offering a number of different optional and types of services throughout the week. In large vibrant churches they were offering services both during the day and in the evenings for those who worked the different shifts. Of course these were large churches that had a number of different types of pastors, but the main senior pastor was truly an overseer of the different ministries; I felt the senior pastor definitely had the gift of administration, a delegator, who was extremely tender to the Voice of the HOLY SPIRIT.

I began to understand the concept of the metropolitan churches I experienced. (1) In large churches who desired being led by the HOLY SPIRIT their worship was at least 45 minutes to an hour or longer and that is not even counting the choir numbers and special songs by individuals; and if the SPIRIT begins to move within the Pastor who understands and follows the leading of the HOLY SPIRIT, then great things begin to happen in that service. Even though the length of the service was longer, it never seemed to feel long because you knew you were in the Presence of Almighty GOD.

But if I would entered a church who did not allowed the HOLY SPIRIT to lead, the service was kept within a ridged format and when you left service my spirit would often feel emptier than it was before I enter into the service. (2) In the different vibrant churches their service would often begin with prayer giving the HOLY SPIRIT control over the service; some would still use the "**The LORD'S Prayer**" or "**The Apostles Creed**," they began with acknowledging the Presence the LORD and having a reverence for HIS Holiness and as the worship service began it would start with up-beat songs of praise and would decrescendo to prepare the people to worship, it was a quieting affect within their spirits, it would also bring the whole body into unity of being in one accord; and (3) then the worship would come to even more of a decrescendo with people singing in the Spirit mixed within the worship songs of the Psalms but those type of songs was where the HOLY SPIRIT was bringing words of songs to flow deep within the hearts of people, when you knew the HOLY SPRIT was directing it to each individual and what they were going through in their present life, yet HE was still ministering to the whole congregation. I realized that the later part of worship was for the preparation for people to receive the Word of GOD and that later worship always inspired the Word to be directed to each individual, as though it was just GOD and you being in one room being in a one to one conversation. This was so different from many other liturgical or denominational churches I attended being governed by man; in the liturgical churches my spirit saw people who were hearing the Word, but often Satan was enticing them to want to point their finger towards this one or another person in the church, saying that it was for them. Through seeing both sides of Church settings, I learned a lot about the importance of true worship as being the preparation of receiving the Word of GOD.

I guess I much desired to be attending larger churches, which were being led by the HOLY SPIRIT for the reason that I did not really get to know the people and their individual problems; I just got to know them by their spirit. I felt as though Satan was truly under our feet and the Power of GOD was so intense that I believe he was fearful of those Powerful Words coming from people of true and powerful worship. This is where I really began to grow in the LORD. Instead of hearing the dos and don'ts, I heard how we can walk by faith, to move mountains, speaking the Promises instead of speaking the problems, experiencing living with the mind of CHRIST. And above all, I learned how to be an Intercessor and the importance of it.

Today, there is such a furious spiritual battle which is taking place that we cannot even see. Another important reason for worship is for the angels that were created by GOD to do battle against demonic spirits and principalities; our intense worship empowers the Warring Angels to strengthened them to do battle. Those angels are called Warriors. Then there are angels that GOD has created just to sit at HIS Throne to continually praise HIM, there are angels that we know of as our guardian angels. In hearing the teachings of GOD'S Word I have learned that GOD has created seven (the perfect number) different types of angels, each with different responsibilities. One of the types of angels, GOD created to come and to usher us into the Kingdom of Heaven to stand before our loving GOD when HE is calling us Home.

As Intercessors, I would advise you to have intercession meetings, you may find that the HOLY SPIRIT may have you spend the entire time in heavy duty worship and singing in the Spirit, on behalf of strengthening the Warring Angels.

Never allow the enemy to make you think that because a service did not follow the common steps: 1, 2, & 3 of many Church services as being incomplete as long as they have allowed the HOLY SPIRIT to be the leader throughout that service. Through my life, I have seen the HOLY SPIRIT turn a whole service around, when a quick Word of the LORD would be at the beginning and the remainder of the service would be nothing but praise and worship; and during the praise and worship you would see people run to the altar, weeping and laying prostrate before the LORD. First time visitors, would just see and watch and their lives would be changed because of the HOLY SPIRIT'S genuine love would touch their inner being, mind and what they were seeing and hearing and show them their ways and they would leave as a different person. I have seen prostitutes change their "**jobs**" by the HOLY SPIRIT convincing them of their ways and HE would then provide good jobs for them. Everyone knew they were all sinners, knowing they were never going to be perfect in this world, but only by the Grace and Mercy of GOD and through the Blood of CHRIST; but they were made perfect in the Eyes of the

FATHER in Heaven. I would feel like I did not want to leave because the Presence of GOD was so strong; people would be slain in the Spirit and healed and set free from their bondages, as burdens would be lifted off of their shoulders – it was awesome to see, yet in these day, we should still expect these things, because we serve an Awesome GOD!

# Prayers of Praise

*"O magnify the LORD with me, and let us lift up HIS Name together." (Psalm 34:3).*

*"As for GOD, HIS way is perfect! The Word of the LORD is tested and try; HE is a Shield to all those who take refuge and put their trust in HIM" (Psalm 18:30).*

*"Let the words of my mouth and the meditation of my heart be acceptable in YOUR sight, O LORD, my firm impenetrable, Rock and my Redeemer" (Psalm 19:14).*

*"Your Word has revived me and given me life" (Psalm 119:50).*

*"Forever, oh LORD, your Word is settled in Heaven" (Psalms 119:89).*

*"Your Word is a lamp to my feet and a Light to my path" (Psalm 119:105*

*"The sum of YOUR Word is truth and every one of YOUR Righteous decrees endures forever" (119:160).*

*"I will worship toward YOUR Holy Temple, and praise YOUR Name for YOUR Loving-kindness and for YOUR Truth and Faithfulness; for YOU are exalted above all else YOUR Name and YOUR Word, and YOU have magnified YOUR Word above all things in YOUR Name!" (Psalm 138:2).*

*"Let my prayer be set forth as incense before YOU, the lifting up of my hands as the evening sacrifice. Set a guard, oh LORD, before my mouth; keep watch at the door of my lips" (Psalm 141:2-3).*

*"He who brings an offering of praise and thanksgiving honors and glorifies ME; and he who orders his way aright—who prepares the way that I may show him—to him I will demonstrate the Salvation of GOD" (Psalm 50:23").*

*"My mouth will be filled with YOUR Praise and with YOUR Honor all day." (Psalm 71:8).*

*"Because YOUR Loving-kindness is better than life, my lips will praise YOU. So will I bless YOU while I live; I will lift up my hands in YOUR Name." (Psalm 63:3-4).*

*"YOUR testimonies are my delight and my counselors." (Psalm 119:24).*

*These Prayers of Praise are taken from the Amplified Bible.*

# Personal Confessions

*"JESUS is LORD over my spirit, my soul, in my body."* (Philippians 2:9-11.)

*"JESUS has made unto me wisdom, righteousness, sanctification, and redeemed. I can do all things through CHRIST, Who strengthens me."* (I Corinthians 1:30, Philippians 4:13.)

*"The LORD is my Shepherd. I will not be in want. My GOD supplies all my needs according to HIS riches in Glory in CHRIST JESUS."* (Psalms 23, Philippians 4:19.)

*"I do not fret or have anxiety about anything. I do not have a care."* (Philippians 4:6, I Peter 5:6-7.)

*"I am part of the Body of CHRIST. I am redeemed from the curse, for JESUS bore my sicknesses and carried my diseases in HIS own Body. By HIS stripes I am healed. I forbid any sickness or disease to operate in my body; for every organ, every tissue of my bodily functions in the perfection in which GOD created it to function. I honor GOD and bring Glory to HIM in my body."* (Galatians 3:13, Matthew 8:17, I Peter 2:24, I Corinthians 6:20.)

*"I have the mind of CHRIST and hold the thoughts, feelings, and purposes of HIS Heart."* (I Corinthians 2:16.)

*"I am a believer and not a doubter. I hold fast to my confession of faith in the Promises of GOD. I have decided to walk by faith and

*practice faith. My faith comes by hearing and hearing by the Word of GOD. JESUS is the Author and the Developer of my faith." (Hebrews 4:14, Hebrews 11:6, Romans 10:17, Hebrews 12:2.)*

*"The Love of GOD has been shed abroad in my heart by the HOLY SPIRIT and HIS Love abides in me richly. I keep myself in the Kingdom of HIS Light, in Love, in the Word, and the wicked one cannot touch me." (Romans 5:5, I John 4:16, I John 5: 18).*

*"I tread upon serpents and scorpions and over all the power of the enemy. I take my Shield of Faith and quench every fiery dart. Greater is HE, Who is in me than he who is in the world." (Psalm 91:13, Ephesians 6:16, I John 4:4).*

*"I am delivered from this present evil world. I am seated with CHRIST in Heavenly places. I reside in the Kingdom of GOD'S dear SON. The law of the Spirit of Life in CHRIST JESUS has made me free from the law of sin and death." (Galatians 1:4, Ephesians 2:6, Colossians 1:13, Romans 8:2.)*

*"I fear not for GOD has given me a Spirit of Power, of Love, and of a sound mind. GOD is on my side." (II Timothy 1:7, Romans 8:31.)*

*"I hear the Voice of the Good Shepherd. I hear my FATHER'S Voice, and the voice of a stranger I will not follow. I roll my works upon the LORD. I commit all my trust completely and wholly unto HIM. HE will cause my thoughts to become agreeable to HIS Will, and so will my plans be established and succeed." (John 10:27, Proverbs 16:3.)*

*"I am in this world, but I am an overcome because I am born of GOD. I represent the FATHER and JESUS in all things. I am a useful member in the Body of CHRIST. I am HIS Workmanship re-created in CHRIST JESUS. My FATHER GOD is all the while effectually at work in me both to will and do HIS good pleasure."* *(I John 5:4-5, Ephesians 2:10, Philippians 2:13.)*

*"I let the Word dwell in me richly. HE who began a good work in me will continue until the Day of CHRIST."* *(Colossians 3:16, Philippians 1:6.)*

# Examples of INTERCESSION Prayers of Faith:

# For our President and the Leaders in our Government

"FATHER, in JESUS Name, I give thanks for our Nation under GOD and its different leaders we have had over our government. We up hold our present leaders in prayer before YOU, calling for them to be as men and women who are in positions of Authority, representing the people of this Nation. We pray and intercede for the President, the Representatives, the Senators, the Judges of our Land, the Armed Forces, the Policemen, the Firemen, as well as the Governors and Mayors, and for all those who are in authority over us in any way. We pray for the SPIRIT of the LORD to rest mightily upon them, convincing them of GOD'S Ways."

"SATAN, WE SPEAK TO YOU, IN THE NAME OF JESUS. WE BIND YOU; YOUR PRINCIPALITIES AND POWERS, THE RULERS OF THE DARKNESS, AND WICKED SPIRITS IN HEAVENLY PLACES, TO TEAR DOWN ANY STRONGHOLDS BEING USED AS MIGHTY WEAPONS; FOR GOD HAS PROVIDED FOR US WEAPONS OF SPIRITUAL WARFARE, IN THE NAME OF JESUS, WITH HIS AUTHORITY AND POWER. GOD HAS GIVEN US THE ABILITY TO BIND UP THE SPIRIT OF THE ANTICHRIST. WE BIND EVERY SPIRIT OF THE

TERRORISTS THROUGHOUT THIS WORLD AND WHO ARE PRESENTLY HIDING IN OUR OWN COUNTRY AND FAMILIAR SPIRITS. WE BIND ANY WORLDLY WISDOM OF ANY FORM–EVERY OPPOSER TO THE TRUTH. WE BIND EVERY DESTRUCTIVE, DECEITFUL, THRIEVING SPIRIT. NOW, IN THE NAME OF JESUS, YOU ARE LOOSENED FROM YOUR ASSIGNMENT AGAINST OUR PRESIDENT AND LEADERS OF THE GOVERNMENT, IN THE NAME OF JESUS, FOR THEY ESCAPE FROM THE SNARE OF THE DEVIL THAT HAS HELD THEM CAPTIVE. GIVING THEM GODLY AUTHORITY AND WISDOM WITH AN ATTITUDE TO BECOME ONE AS LEADERS OF THIS NATION."

"We believe that skillful and GODLY Wisdom has entered into the heart of our President and knowledge is pleasant to him. Discretion watches over him; understanding keeps him and delivers him from the way of the evil one and from evil people with bad decisions. He thinks and receives counsel from GODLY advisers, who are committed to the Wisdom of GOD.

FATHER, we state that YOU surround the President with YOUR Angels and with men and women who make their hearts and ears attentive to GODLY counsel and do that which is right in YOUR sight. We believe YOU can cause them to be men and women of integrity, who are obedient concerning the people they represent, that through the Power of Prayer, they will be lead in a quiet and a peaceful life of harmony in all GODLINESS and Honesty. We pray that the upright will dwell in our government… that they are men and women blameless and complete in YOUR sight. FATHER shield these positions with YOUR Authority; but the wicked individuals will be cut off and be remove from their governmental positions, who do not observe YOUR GODLY Ways. May those ungodly Representatives be pulled out by the roots of their leadership. We call all people who are in authority in this country to walk uprightly, continually being convinced by the HOLY SPIRIT that their walk and decisions are directed completely from YOU, the Most High GOD, as they truly have the heart of the people in their minds as they make their decisions.

YOUR Word declares that 'Blessed is the Nation whose GOD is the LORD...' We receive your blessings. FATHER, YOU are their Refuge and Stronghold in times of trouble (inflation, recession, destitution and desperation). So we declare with our mouths that your people dwell safely in this land and we will prosper in YOUR abundance. We are more than conquerors through CHRIST JESUS!

It is written in YOUR Word as it states, ***"The heart of the kings are in the Hand of the LORD and HE will cause the waters to turn which way HE desires."*** (Proverbs 21:1). Therefore according to GOD'S Word, we believe the hearts of our leaders are in YOUR Hand and that their decisions are divinely directed by the YOU.

We give thanks unto YOU that the Good News of the Gospel is published in our land. The Word of the LORD prevails and grows mightily in the hearts and lives of the people. We thank YOU that this Nation and the Leaders YOU have in their seats will be people of integrity always keeping in mind that they are to represent the people of this Nation, in JESUS Name." **"JESUS is LORD over the United States!"**

## SCRIPTURE REFERENCES:

| | |
|---|---|
| I Timothy 2:1-3 | Deuteronomy 28:10, 11 |
| | Proverbs 2:10-12, 21, 22 |
| Romans 8:37 | Psalms 33:12 |
| | Proverbs 21:1 |
| Psalms 9:9 | Acts 12:24 |

# For Nations and Continents

"FATHER, in the Name of JESUS, we bring before YOU the Countries and their Leaders to come in line with YOUR Word. FATHER, YOU said in YOUR Word that YOU would reprove Leaders for our sakes so we may live a quiet and peaceful life in all GODLINESS and honesty.

We pray that skillful and GODLY Wisdom has entered into their hearts as Leaders and that YOUR Knowledge is pleasant to them; that discretion watches over them and understanding keeps them and delivers them from evil ways and from the evil one.

We pray that upright Leaders will dwell in all governing bodies, with men and women of integrity, blameless and complete in YOUR Sight; FATHER, in JESUS' Name, we call them to remain steadfast in the leading of the HOLY SPIRIT; but the wicked will be cut out of these different governments, who are the individuals who are bringing forth havoc and chaos, having these treacherous individuals to be rooted out of their position and replaced people of honor and respect for the people in their Nations. We pray that those in authority have discernment in removing those who are wicked from among the good and bring the threshing wheel over them to separate the chaff from the grain with YOUR Loving-kindness and mercy, truth, faithfulness preserve those with a right heart to remain in authority, and their office is upheld by the people's loyalty.

We confess and believe that the decisions made by their leaders are divinely directed by YOU, FATHER, and their mouth will not transgress in judgment. Therefore, the Leaders are men and women of discernment, understanding, and knowledge so the stability of these Leaders in the different countries will continue to grow strong in YOUR Wisdom and Knowledge and continue in doing well. We pray that the uncompromising righteous be in authority, so the people can rejoice and be blessed in abundance.

FATHER, it is an abomination to YOU and for leaders to commit wickedness and that those leaders of wickedness will be up-rooted and pulled out of the place of leadership and be replaced with Leaders with upright hearts. We pray that their office be established and made secure by YOUR Righteousness, that right and just lips are a delight to those in authority, so they will speak what is right and just.

We pray and believe that Good News of the Gospel is published in their Nations. We thank YOU for laborers of the harvest; to publish YOUR Word, that JESUS is LORD in of their lives. We thank you for raising up intercessors to pray for them, in JESUS Name. Amen"

## SCRIPTURES REFERENCES:

| | | |
|---|---|---|
| Psalm 105:14 | Proverbs 28:2 | Proverbs 2:10-15 |
| Proverbs 29:2 | Proverbs 2:21-22 | I Timothy 2:1-2 |
| Proverbs 20:26, 28 | Acts 12:24 | Proverbs 21:1 |
| Psalm 68:11 | Proverbs 16:10, 12, 13 | |

# For the School Systems
## (Authority, Children and Parent)

"FATHER, we thank you for the reality of YOUR Word which brings forth YOUR Light and Knowledge. I thank YOU that YOU watch over YOUR Word to perform it. FATHER, we bring before YOU the _____ school system(s) and the men and women who are in positions of Authority within the school system(s).

We believe they are skillful and have GODLY Wisdom within their hearts and minds; that YOUR Knowledge is pleasing to them. We declare YOUR discretion watches over them; and YOUR understanding keeps them and delivers them from the evil ways. We pray that our teachers will be of great integrity, blameless and complete in YOUR sight, so they remain in these positions. We also call forth protection so all wicked concepts to be cut off and the treacherous teaching be rooted out, in the Name of JESUS. FATHER, we thank YOU for **born-again, Spirit-filled teachers and leaders** to be put into these positions.

FATHER, we bring our children, our young people _____ before YOU. FATHER, we speak forth YOUR Word for them to have YOUR boldness and confidence as they bring that concept within each of their homes, declaring each household to have parents who engage themselves in helping their children to do well in school. We are redeemed from the curse of the law all because JESUS was made a curse for us. **Our sons and daughters are not given to another people.** We enjoy our children, and they will not be caught into any form of captivity or bondage, in the Name of JESUS. We call our children and young people to become leaders and not to be given into peer pressure or bullied by others. We call that they are respectful, but bold and walk in YOUR Authority.

We call the parents to be responsible parents to train and teach their children in the way they should go, and when they are old they will not depart from it.

We call our children to be strong and of good courage and to shy away from whatever might offend YOU, FATHER, or discredit the Name of CHRIST. They show themselves to be blameless, guileless, and uncontaminated children of GOD without blemish (faultless) in the midst of a crooked and wicked generation; holding on to the Promises of GOD'S Word of Life. Thank YOU, FATHER that YOU are filling them with knowledge and skills in all learning YOUR Wisdom; and bringing them in favor with those around them.

FATHER, we pray and intercede for these young people _____, their parents' _____, and the leaders in the school system(s) _____ to separate themselves from being in contact with contaminating and corrupting influences. They cleanse themselves from everything that would contaminate and defile their spirit, mind, and body. We bind the enemy from coming near them and loose the ability by having discernment to be bold as they learn to shun immorality and all sexual looseness—flee from impure thoughts, in word, or deed. They live and conduct themselves honorably and becomingly as in the open light of day. We confess that they shun youthful lust and flee from them, in the Name of JESUS."

"SATAN, WE SPEAK TO YOU IN THE NAME OF JESUS. WE BIND YOU, THE PRINCIPALITIES, THE POWERS, THE RULERS OF THE DARKNESS, AND WICKED SPIRITS IN HEAVENLY PLACES AND TEAR DOWN STRONGHOLDS USING THE MIGHTY WEAPONS GOD HAS PROVIDED FOR US, IN THE NAME OF JESUS. WE BIND UP THAT SPIRIT OF ANTICHRIST. WE BIND EVERY SPIRIT OF THE OCCULT–ASTROLOGY, WITCHCRAFT, AND EVERY UNFAMILIAR SPIRIT. WE BIND THE SEXUAL DESIRES AS YOUNG PEOPLE, IDOLATRY, OBSCENITY, AND PROFANITY. WE BIND THOSE SPIRITS OF ALCOHOL, NICOTINE, AND DRUG ADDICTION. WE BIND WORLDLY CONCEPTS IN ANY FORM AND EVERY OPPOSER TO THE TRUTH. WE BIND EVERY DESTRUCTIVE, DECEITFUL, THREIVING SPIRIT. SATAN, YOU ARE LOOSE FROM YOUR ASSIGNMENT AGAINST _____, IN THE NAME OF JESUS FOR THEY ESCAPE FROM THE SNARE OF THE DEVIL THAT HAS HELD THEM CAPTIVE."

"We commissioned the ministering spirits to go forth and police the areas of our schools, dispelling the forces of darkness.

FATHER, we thank YOU that in CHRIST, all the treasures of Divine Wisdom (of comprehensive insight into the ways and purposes of GOD), and all riches of spiritual knowledge and enlightenment are stored up and lie hidden for them as they learn to walk in HIM. We bind the spirit that distorts our young people with the attitude that they lack the ability to achieve. For YOUR Word says, "**I can do all things through CHRIST, Who strengthens me**;" our children walk in all wisdom and are the head and not the tail; having a sound mind.

We praise YOU, FATHER, that we will see _____ walking with respect and virtue, revering YOUR Name, FATHER. JESUS, those who err in spirit will come to the understanding and those who murmur discontentedly will accept instruction to do YOUR Will and carry out YOUR purposes in their lives for YOUR Glory, FATHER, occupy first place in their hearts. We surround them with GOD'S Word to build up their faith.

Thank YOU, FATHER, that YOU are the delivering GOD. Thank YOU, for the Good News of the Gospel that is published through the lives of our young people, for they are the Living Word in our school system(s). Thank YOU for intercessors to stand on YOUR Word and for laborers of the harvest to preach YOUR Word in JESUS' Name as they are being taught by well-educated by spiritual oriented teachers, who are sensitive to their students' needs. We praise the LORD!"

## SCRIPTURES REFERENCES:

| | | |
|---|---|---|
| Psalm 119:130 | I Corinthians 6:18 | Jeremiah 1:12 |
| Romans 13:13 | Proverbs 2:10-12 | Ephesians 5:4 |
| Proverbs 2:21, 22 | II Timothy 2:22 | The Acts 16:31 |
| Matthew 18:18 | Galatians 3:13 | II Timothy 2:26 |
| Deuteronomy 28:32,41 | Hebrews 1:14 | Proverbs 22:6 |
| Colossians 2:3 | Philippians 2:15,16 | Isaiah 29:23, 24 |
| Daniel 1:17, 9 | I John 2:17 | II Timothy 2:21 |
| I John 5:21 | II Corinthians 7:1 | |

# For the Body of CHRIST

"FATHER, we pray and confess YOUR Word over the Body of CHRIST. We pray they will be filled with the full (deep and clear) Knowledge of YOUR Will in all Spiritual Wisdom—that gives them a comprehensive insight into YOUR Ways and Purposes of GOD and in Understanding with Discernment of Spiritual Things; that they will walk and live, conducting themselves in a manner worthy of YOU, LORD, fully pleasing to YOU and desiring to please YOU in all things, bearing fruit in every good work which continues to be steadily growing and is increasing in and by the Knowledge of YOU— with a fuller, deeper and clearer insights, having acquaintance and recognition of the Voice of the HOLY SPIRIT.

We pray for the Body of CHRIST to be invigorated and strengthened with all power, according to the might of YOUR Glory, to exercise every kind of endurance and patience (perseverance and forbearance) with joy, giving thanks to YOU, FATHER, Who has qualified and made them fit to share the portion which is the inheritance of all the saints (GOD'S holy people), who live in the Light of JESUS. YOU, FATHER, have delivered and drawn us to YOURSELF, making YOU to be in control over all the dominion of darkness and have transferred them into the Kingdom of the SON of Your Love, in whom they have their redemption through HIS blood, which means the remission of their sins.

FATHER, YOU are delighted at the sight of the Body of CHRIST standing shoulder to shoulder in such orderly array and the firmness and the solid front and steadiness of their faith in CHRIST—that leans upon YOUR Characteristics, having an absolute trust and confidence in YOUR Power, Wisdom, and Goodness. They—regulate their lives and conduct themselves—in union and conformity to HIM, evaluating the roots of their spiritual being so it is firm, steady and deeply planted in HIM—fixed and founded in HIM—being continually built up in HIM, becoming increasingly more earned, and estimated in their faith.

FATHER, YOUR people, clothe themselves as your own picked representatives, YOUR chosen ones, who are purified, holy and well-beloved by YOU putting on behavior marked by tender-hearted pity and mercy, kind feelings, gentle ways and patience—which is tireless, long-suffering and have the power to endure whatever comes, with a good temper. Gentle and forgiving with each other and, if they have a differences (a grievance or complaint) against another, they are ready to pardon each other; even as YOU, LORD have freely given to us, so do they also forgive.

YOUR people put on love and enfold themselves with the bond of perfectness— which binds everything together completely in an ideal harmony. They let that peace from JESUS' example be as an umpire continually within their hearts—deciding and settling with all finality all the questions that arise in their minds − space in that peaceful state to which they are called. They are thankful, appreciative, always giving praise to YOU.

The Body of CHRIST lets the Word spoken by CHRIST, the MESSIAH, have its home in their hearts and minds and dwells in them in all richness, as they teach, admonish, and train each other in all insight, intelligence, and wisdom and spiritual songs, making melody to YOU, FATHER, with YOUR Grace in their hearts.

And whatever they do in word or deed, they do everything in the Name of the LORD JESUS and in dependence upon HIS Person, giving praise to YOU, FATHER, through HIM!"

## SCRIPTURE REFERENCES:
Colossians 1:9-14    Colossians 3:12-17    Colossians 2:5-7

# Pray for Jerusalem

"FATHER in obedience to YOUR Word we pray for the peace of Jerusalem according to: (Psalm 122:5 – "**Pray for the peace of Jerusalem: 'May they prosper who love YOU.'** ") But FATHER, I carefully pray because the special event that took place years ago in making the past decisions which have now affected the present region of the Middle East. We call forth your love to overcome their difference and learn from past mistakes to have forgiveness and respect for each other as GOD'S people, therefore, nurture their spirits as Nations under GOD. Psalm 122 declares the example of having true worship in YOUR temple in Jerusalem.

"SATAN, I BIND YOU FROM STEALING AND CONVERTING WHAT GOD HAS CREATED AS GOOD. FOR YOU HAVE DEGRADED ITS MAN-GIVEN NAME CALLED 'RELIGION'. I THEREFORE BIND YOUR TERM OF THE FUNDALMENTAL RELIGIONS THAT YOU HAVE FILLED WITH BITTERNESS, HATRED, LIES, JEALOUSY, ENVY, GREED, OUTBURST OF WRATH, SELFISH AMBITIONS, DISSENSIONS, HERESIES, REVELRY AND ANY AND ALL THINGS THAT GO AGAINST WHAT JESUS FOUGHT AGAINST THE SCRIBES , PHARISEES AND SADDUCEES IN THE DAYS OF OLD. I BIND YOUR ACT OF CONVEYING THAT SAME SPIRIT WITHIN THE CHURCHES TODAY AND I LOOSE TRUE WORSHIP TO THE LIVING GOD; I CALL GOD'S PEOPLE TO FLOW WITH THE FRUITS OF THE SPIRIT: LOVE, JOY, PEACE, LONGSUFFERING, KINDNESS,

GOODNESS, FAITHFULNESS, GENTLENESS, AND SELF-CONTROL. I LOOSE GODLY WISDOM TO THE LEADERS OF THESE ARGUING COUNTRIES. FATHER, I DECLARE THESE ACTS DONE, IN JESUS NAME."

FATHER, I declare that the HOLY SPIRIT divides the GOD'S WORD, both the Old Testament and the New Testament, so that the Word of GOD thwarts every act of the enemy, so healing and peace will rise up in the Middle Eastern, between the differences of "**religions**." I call forth healing to the present generations because of the dissension that has brought havoc from years ago between Ishmael and Isaac. FATHER, I call forth a HOLY GHOST revival to cover the Middle East as a cloud, thwarting the enemy's plan, in JESUS Name. GOD has called Jerusalem to be the example of a true place of worship to the Living GOD regardless how the man-made term of "**religion**" exists!

**FATHER, GOD, we ask that YOU take control to rule over the Middle East! Hallelujah! Amen!**

## SCRIPTURE REFERENCES:

Psalm 122:5 – *"Pray for the peace of Jerusalem: 'May they prosper who love you." [Pray–Sha'al: is to ask, inquire, request, pray, desire, wish for, demand. Sha'al is not the usual Hebrew work for "pray," but it has the suggestion of "asking for" or "inquiring about" something. In this psalm for the sake of GOD'S people and for the sake of the LORD's house we are instructed to seek Jerusalem's good, that is, to inquire earnestly about its welfare, pray for peace and ask with true concern about its condition. The proper name of sha'al is* **Sha'ul** *(Saul) meaning "Asked for" or "Requested," that is to say, a wanted child.]*

Jeremiah 1:12         Isaiah 61:9           Hosea 3:5
Genesis 12:3          Hebrews 7:22         Romans 11:14 & 23

Isaiah    60:1                      Matthew    18:18

Isaiah 55:11-12 – *"(11) So will MY word be that goes forth from MY mouth; It will not return to ME void. But it will accomplish what I please, and it will prosper in the thing for which I sent it. (12) For you will go out with joy, and be led out with peace; the mountains and the hills will break forth into singing before you, and all the trees of the field will clap their hands."*

Hebrews 7:25 – *"Therefore He is also able to save to the uttermost those who come to GOD through Him, since He always live to make intercession for them."*

Psalm 130:7 – *"O Israel, hope in the LORD; for with the LORD there is mercy, and with Him is abundant redemption."*

Isaiah 52:9 – *"Break forth into joy, sing together; you wasted places of Jerusalem! For the LORD has comforted HIS people, HE has redeemed Jerusalem."*

# For Ministers and Ministries

"FATHER, in the Name of JESUS, we pray and confess that the SPIRIT of the LORD rests upon YOUR anointed pastors, as overseers of your sheep, who are filled with the Spirit of Wisdom and Understanding, the Spirit of Counsel and Might, the Spirit of Knowledge, the Spirit of Administration. We also pray that YOUR SPIRIT rests upon the pastors to be of quick to understand because YOU, LORD, have anointed and qualified them to preach the gospel to the needy, the poor, the wealthy, and the afflicted. We call them to be filled or actively desiring all the gifts you have empowered to the Body of CHRIST. We call that they have an inner sensitivity to each individual's situation that will cause them to be filled with YOUR Love and Compassion as JESUS displayed; for you have called them and sent them to break the Bread of Life, feed the hunger hearted and heal the brokenhearted, to proclaim liberty to the physical and the spiritual activists, and to release those who have imprisoned themselves with bad habits and use them to open the eyes of those who are bound. I call a HOLY GHOST revival to fall upon our pastors, enlightened to the Word of GOD as never before. They will walk in Truth with Understanding that the enemy cannot thwart. The enemy shall know them by name and fear what comes from their mouths, for their mouths are filled with the Promises of GOD that will cause the enemy to flee seven ways and to pierce the heart of man with love by the Two-edged Sword. This Word will cause man to run to hear the Word and create a hunger to see the Promises of GOD fulfilled.

We pray and believe according to the Scriptures that no weapon formed against any and all pastors will prosper and that any tongue that rises up against them in judgment will be shown to be in the wrong. We pray that YOU cause YOUR anointed pastors to prosper abundantly, LORD–physically, spiritually and financially.

We confess that YOUR anointed pastors know how to hold fast and follow the pattern of wholesome and sound teaching in all faith and love which is for us in CHRIST JESUS. We call forth all pastors to have the mind of CHRIST, to be extremely sensitive to the moving and obedience to the leading of the HOLY SPIRIT. YOUR anointed pastors are guarded and kept with the greatest love, by the precious and excellently adapted Truth which has been entrusted to them through the HOLY SPIRIT Who makes HIS home in their lives.

LORD, we pray and believe that, each and every day, freedom of utterance is poured as Holy Oil on each pastor as they open their mouth boldly and courageously, speaking forth the Word as they ought to do to minister the gospel to the people. Thank you, LORD, for the added strength which comes with YOUR Greatness that YOU have given to each pastor.

We hereby confess that we will stand behind our pastors and undergird them in prayer. We will speak positive words with our mouths that will edify our pastors. As intercessors, we declare before YOU, LORD, that any negative act or belief that we see or hear that contradicts the Holy Scriptures will fall as before deaf ears, and declare that only the

Promises will be heard through the ears and poured into the deepest parts of their hearts and minds.

We will not allow ourselves to judge the pastors, but to continue to intercede for them; calling forth through the Power of Pray, blessings upon them, in the Name of JESUS. Thank you, JESUS, for the answers. Hallelujah!"

## SCRIPTURE REFERENCES:

| | | |
|---|---|---|
| Isaiah 11:2, 3 | II Timothy 1:13, 14 | Isaiah 61:1, 6 |
| Ephesians 6:19, 20 | Isaiah 54:17 | I Peter 3:12 |

# For Missionaries

"FATHER, we lift before YOU those in the Body of CHRIST who are out in the different fields of this world and are bringing the Good News of the Gospel—not only in this country but also around the world. We lift those in the Body of CHRIST who are suffering persecution—those who are in prison for their beliefs and teaching the Good News of JESUS CHRIST. FATHER, we know that YOU watch over YOUR Word to perform it, that YOUR Word prospers in what YOU have declared it to perform. Therefore, we speak YOUR Word and establish YOUR Covenant on this earth. We pray they will receive the answers of YOUR desires through the HOLY SPIRIT.

Thank YOU, FATHER, for revealing unto YOUR people the integrity of YOUR Word that through YOU, they will be firm, strong and steadfast in faith against the devil's onset, withstanding him. FATHER, YOU are their Light, Salvation, Refuge, and Stronghold. YOU hide them in YOUR Shelter and set them high upon the Rock. It is YOUR Will that each will prosper, be in good health, and lived in victory. YOU have set prisoners free, fed the hungry, executed justice, rescued, and delivered.

"SATAN, WE BIND YOU AND EVERY MENACING SPIRIT THAT WOULD STIR UP AGAINST GOD'S PEOPLE, IN JESUS NAME; AND LOOSEN THE POWER OF GOD'S WILL TO BE PERFORMED ACCORDING TO HIS WILL."

"We commissioned the ministering spirits to go forth and provide the necessary help for and assistance to YOUR heirs of Salvation. For we are strong in the LORD and in the Power of YOUR Might, quenching every fiery dart of the devil, in JESUS' Name.

FATHER, we call forth the Blood of JESUS to cover the Missionaries, in the Body of CHRIST, with YOUR Word. We say that no weapon formed against them will prosper and any negative tongue that rises against them will be cast down; for YOU are the Great Judge, Who will show forth YOUR Righteousness in YOUR Children. This peace, security, and triumph over opposition are their inheritance as YOUR children. This is the righteousness which they obtain from YOU, FATHER, which YOU have imparted to be their justification. They are far from even the thought of destruction, for they will not be fearful of any terror that may come near them.

FATHER, YOU promised that YOU will establish YOUR children to the end, keeping them steadfast, giving them strength, and giving them the guarantee of any form of vindication, that is, be their warrant against all accusations or indictment. They are not anxious beforehand how they will reply in defense or what they are to say for the HOLY SPIRIT will instruct them in that very hour and moment what they ought to say to those in the outside world, their speech being seasoned with salt.

We commit these brothers and sisters in the LORD to YOU, FATHER, deposited into YOUR charge, entrusting them to YOUR Protection and care, for YOU are faithful. YOU strengthen them, set them on a firm foundation, and guard them from the evil one. We join our voices with high praise to YOU, Most High GOD, and silence the enemy and avenger. Praise the LORD! Greater is HE Who is in us then he who is in the world!" (*High praise is singing in the spirit.*)

**SCRIPTURE REFERENCES**:

| | | |
|---|---|---|
| Jeremiah 1:12 | Ephesians 6:10, 16 | Isaiah 55:11 |
| Isaiah 54:14, 17 | I Peter 5:9 | I Corinthians 1:8 |
| Psalm 27:1, 5 | Luke 12:11-12 | III John 2 |
| Colossians 4:6 | I John 5:4-5 | Acts 20:32 |
| Psalm 146:7 | II Thessalonians 3:3 | Psalm 144:7 |
| Psalm 8:2 | Matthew 18:18 | I John 4:4 |
| | Hebrews 1:14 | |

# For Meetings, Seminars and Bible Studies

"FATHER, in the Name of JESUS, we openly confess that the Word of GOD will come forth boldly and accurately during these and all (*meetings*) and that the people who hear YOUR Word will not be able to resist the intelligence, the wisdom and the inspiration of the HOLY SPIRIT that will be spoken through YOUR ministers and teachers of the Gospel.

We confess that, as YOUR Word goes forth, an anointing of the HOLY SPIRIT will cause people to open their spiritual eyes and ears and turn from darkness to the Light—from the power of Satan, to YOU, GOD; and allow JESUS to be their LORD.

We commit these meetings to YOU, FATHER, deposited it into YOUR charge—entrusting these meetings, so the people will hear, and they will declare YOUR protection and care. We commend these meetings to come in alignment of YOUR True Word— the commands, counsels, and promises of YOUR unmerited favor. FATHER, we know that YOUR Word will build up the people and caused them to realize that they are joint heirs with JESUS.

We believe, FATHER, that is YOUR Word comes forth through the anointing of YOUR speaker and will be controlled completely by the HOLY SPIRIT for the Word of GOD that is spoken is Alive and full of Power, making it active, operative, energizing, and effective, be as being sharper than any Two-edged Sword. We declare that the inner ear of every believer and unbeliever will clearly hear so that every need of every person will be met spiritually, physically, mentally, financially.

We thank YOU, FATHER, and praise YOU that, because we have asked and agree together, these petitions have and will come to pass. Let these words which we have made supplication before the LORD, be near to the LORD our GOD day and night, that HE may maintain their cause and right of HIS people and (*meeting*s) as each of it requires! We believe all the earth's people will know that the LORD is GOD and there is no other! Hallelujah!"

## SCRIPTURE REFERENCES:

| | | |
|---|---|---|
| James 5:16 | Acts 26:18 | Matthew 18:19 |
| Acts 20:32 | Ephesians 6:19 | Hebrews 4:12 |
| Acts 6:10 | Philadelphians 4:19 | Ephesians 1:18 |
| | I Kings 8:59-60 | |

# Prosperity for Ministering Servants

"FATHER, how we praise and thank YOU for YOUR Word knowing that YOU Watch over YOUR Word to perform it and no Word of YOURS will return void, but it shall accomplishes that which YOU please, knowing it will prosper in what we ask according to YOUR Word for which YOU gave to us.

FATHER, in the Name of JESUS, we pray, confess and believe according to YOUR Word that those in YOUR Body who have sown good spiritual seed of among the people which will reap from the people's material benefits for LORD which YOU have directed to those who publish the Good News of the Gospel should live and get their maintenance by the Gospel. We confess that YOUR ministers and teachers to seek and are eager for the fruit which increases to the people's credit–the harvest of blessings that are accumulating within their account. The people's gifts are as a fragrant incence as an offering, a sacrifice which YOU, FATHER welcome, and are delighted. You will liberally supply, fill to the fullness, YOUR peoples' every needs according to YOUR riches in Glory in CHRIST JESUS.

We confess that those who receive instruction in the Word of GOD will be quick to share all good things with their teachers, contributing to their support. We confess that YOUR people will not lose heart nor grow weary and not faint in acting nobly–for they will reap YOUR blessings; but if they do lose heart and relax in their courage, they will faint. So then, as occasion and opportunity comes to them; causing them to open their hearts as unto belief as people of GOD, so they will do good to all people not only being useful and profitable to them, but also doing what is for their spiritual good and advantage.

We confess for YOUR people to be a blessing in whatever they touch will be blessed, especially to those of the household of faith– those who belong to GOD'S family, the Believers. Therefore, we believe and confess that YOUR people will sow the Word generously in order for YOUR blessings to be poured out upon them. YOUR people will then reap generously and with blessings from YOU, Almighty GOD, Who is full of love; therefore, take pleasure in and receive the prize above all things. But those who are willing but feel abandoned, may raise them up so within their spirits will allow them to become doers with a cheerful, joyous; prompt-to-do-it giver–whose heart is in his giving. GOD, YOU are then able to make all Grace, every favor and earthly blessing, come to YOUR people in abundance, so they are always and under all circumstances and whatever the need, self-sufficient, possessing enough to require no aid or support and furnished in abundance for every good work and charitable donation.

As YOUR people give, their deeds of justice, goodness, kindness, benevolence go forward and endure forever. And GOD, YOU, Who provide the seed for the sower and bread for eating, will also provide and multiply the people's resources for sowing and increase the fruits of their Righteousness in the work of faith. Therefore, YOUR people are enriched in all things and in every way so they can be generous and their generosity as it is administered by YOUR teachers in bringing thanksgiving to GOD.

As it is written, *'Give and it will be given to you, good measure, pressed down, shaken together and running over will men pour into your life. For with the measure you deal out it will be measured back to you.'* Praise the LORD!"

## SCRIPTURE REFERENCES:

Jeremiah 1:12  Galatians 6:6-10  Isaiah 55:11
II Corinthians 9:6-11  I Corinthians 9:11, 14  Luke 6:38
Philippians 4:17-19

# To Be GOD-inside Minded

"I am a spirit, I have a soul and a sound mind, and I live in a physical body. My spirit is the Candle of the LORD. GOD, my FATHER, is guiding me into all Truth through my spirit.

I am a child of GOD, born of the SPIRIT of GOD, filled with the SPIRIT of GOD, and led by the SPIRIT. I listen to my heart as I allow the HOLY SPIRIT to see that my spirit is upright within me.

The HOLY SPIRIT gives direction to my spirit and revelation to my mind. HE leads me in the way I should go in all the affairs of my life. HE leads me by an inward witness. The eyes of my understanding are being enlightened. Wisdom is in my inward parts. HIS Love is perfected in me. I have an anointing from the HOLY SPIRIT to act and be an asset to HIS Kingdom.

I am becoming spirit-conscious. I listen to the Voice of the SPIRIT and obey what the SPIRIT tells me. I let HIS SPIRIT dominate me, for I walk not after the flesh, but after the SPIRIT. I examine myself to be assured that I am being leading in the Light of HIS Word. I trust in the LORD with all my heart and lean not to my own understanding. In all my ways I acknowledge HIM, and HE directs my paths. I walk in the Light of GOD'S Word.

**"I will educate and train and develop my human spirit according to the Word of GOD.** The Word of GOD will not depart out of my mouth until I am led to speak. I mediate within the Word day and night. Therefore it will make my way prosperous, and I will have great success in life. **I am a doer of the Word as I put GOD'S Word first.** My spirit man is in controlled by the SPIRIT.

*"Thanks be unto GOD, Who always causes me to triumph in CHRIST!"*

## SCRIPTURE REFERENCES:

| | | |
|---|---|---|
| I Thessalonians 5:23 | Job 38:36 | Proverbs 20:27 |
| I John 4:12 | John 16:13 | I John 2:20 |
| Romans 8:14, 16 | Romans 9:1 | John 3:6-7 |
| Romans 8:1 | John 7:37-39 | Proverbs 3:5-6 |
| Ephesians 5:18 | Psalm 119:105 | Isaiah 48:17 |
| Joshua 1:8 | Ephesians 1:18 | James 1:22 |
| I Corinthians 1:30 | II Corinthians 2:14 | |

# For GOD'S Word and an Accurate Prayer Life

"FATHER, in the Name of JESUS, **I commit myself to walk according to the Word.** Since YOUR Word is living within me, it will produce YOUR Light with in this world. I recognize that YOUR Word is integrity itself—steadfast, sure, eternal—and I trust my life to its provisions.

You have sent YOUR Word forth into the forefront of my heart. I let it dwell within me, richly in all wisdom. I meditate in it day and night so I may diligently respond to its instructions. The Incorruptible Seed, the Living Word, the Word of Truth, is abiding in my spirit. That Seed is growing mightily in me now, producing YOUR Nature, YOUR Life and Character. It is my counsel, my shield, my buckler, my powerful weapon in battle. The Word is a Lamp to my feet and a Light to my path. It makes my way to become easy before me. So I will not stumble, for my steps are ordered by the LORD.

The HOLY SPIRIT leads and guides me into all the truth. HE gives me understanding, discernment, and comprehension so I am preserved from the snares of the evil one.

FATHER, YOUR Eyes are over the Righteous. Therefore, YOUR Ears are open to my prayers. **I am a person of prayer**—my prayers are rooted in YOUR Word. **I do make time to pray**. I am earnest, unwearied, and steadfast in my prayer life, being both alert and intent in my praying with thanksgiving. I am an intercessor—a prayer warrior, strong in the power of YOUR Might. I refuse to turn cowardly—or faint, losing heart, nor will I give up, for **my prayers avail much**, in the Name of JESUS.

I delight myself in YOU and YOUR Word. Because of that, YOU put YOUR desires within my heart. I commit my ways unto YOU and YOU bring them to pass. I am confident that YOU are at work within me now both to will and to do all YOUR good pleasures.

I exalt YOUR Word, hold it in high esteem, and give it FIRST place. **I make my schedule around YOUR Word;** I make the Word to be the final authority to settle all questions that confront me. I choose to agree with the Word of GOD; and choose to disagree with any thoughts, conditions, or circumstances contrary to YOUR Word. I boldly and confidently say that my heart is fixed and established on the solid foundation—the Rock of JESUS CHRIST, the Living Word of GOD!"

**SCRIPTURE REFERENCES:**

| | | |
|---|---|---|
| Hebrews 4:12 | I Peter 3:12 | Colossians 3:16 |
| Colossians 4:2 | Joshua 1:8 | Ephesians 6:10 |
| I Peter 1:23 | Luke 18:1 | Psalm 91:4 |
| James 5:16 | Psalm 119:105 | Psalm 37:4, 5 |
| Psalm 37:23 | Philippians 2:13 | Colossians 1:9 |
| II Corinthians 10:5 | John 16:13 | Psalm 112:7, 8 |

# To Rejoice in the LORD

"FATHER, this is the day the LORD has made. I rejoice and I am glad in it! I always find joy in rejoicing in YOU. And again I say, I rejoice. I delight myself in YOU, LORD. Happy am I who's GOD is the LORD!

FATHER, YOU said YOU rejoice over me with a joy that is constantly overflowing. Hallelujah! I rejoice for I am redeemed by the Blood of the Lamb. I come with singing, and YOUR everlasting joy is upon my head. I obtain joy, gladness; for sorrow and sighing will flee away. The spirit of rejoicing, joy, and laughter is my heritage. When the Spirit of the LORD is within me there is liberty—I am set free from any form of bondage and I walk in the Liberty of YOUR freedom.

FATHER, my mouth will praise YOU with joyful lips. I am forever filled and stimulated by the HOLY SPIRIT. I speak and sing out in psalms and hymns, making melody with all my heart to YOU, as my LORD. My happy heart is a good like medicine and my cheerful mind brings forth healing within my body. The light in my eyes rejoices with the hearts of others. I have a good report. My countenance radiates with the Joy of the LORD.

FATHER, I thank YOU for the fruit I call forth through prayer. I ask in JESUS' Name, and I will receive it so my joy (gladness, delight) is full, complete, and overflowing. **For the joy of the LORD is my strength.** Therefore, I can count it all joy, all strength; even when I encounter tests or trials of any other sort; I am strong in YOU, FATHER.

I have the victory in the Name of JESUS. Satan is under my feet. I am not moved by adverse circumstances. I have been made the Righteous before GOD as I work my faith in CHRIST JESUS. I dwell in the Kingdom of GOD and have peace and joy in the HOLY SPIRIT! Praise the LORD!"

## SCRIPTURE REFERENCES:

| | | |
|---|---|---|
| Psalm 118:24 | Philippians 4:4 | Philippians 3:1 |
| Psalm 144:15 | Zephaniah 3:17 | Isaiah 51:11 |
| II Corinthians 3:17 | James 1:25 | Psalm 63:5 |
| Ephesians 5:18-19 | Proverbs 17:22 | Proverbs 15:30 |
| Philippians 4:8 | Proverbs 15:13 | John 15:7, 8 |
| John 16:23 | Nehemiah 8:10 | James 1:2 |
| Ephesians 6:10 | I John 5:4 | Ephesians 1:22 |
| II Corinthians 5:7 | II Corinthians 5:21 | Romans 14:17 |

# To Walk in GOD'S Wisdom and His Perfect Will

"SATAN, IN JESUS' NAME, WE RELEASE YOU FROM YOUR ASSIGNMENT OF TAMPERING WITH _____'S MIND AND THOUGHTS AS GOD'S CHILD FOR HE WALKS IN GODLY WISDOM AND UNDERSTANDING ACCORDINGING TO PROVERBS 9:10. _____ WALKS ACCORDING TO THE WILL OF THE FATHER AND IS LED BY THE HOLY SPIRIT; THEREFORE, YOU HAVE NO AUTHORITY OVER _____'S MIND, THOUGHTS, AND THE MAKING OF DECISIONS. *HE* HAS A SOUND MIND AND THE MIND SET WHICH IS IMPARTED FROM ALMIGHTY GOD; THEREFORE, SATAN YOU MUST TAKE YOUR HANDS OFF _____. AS INTERCESSORS, WE BIND YOU FROM *HIS* LIFE. IN JESUS' NAME, I COMMAND YOU TO IMMEDIATELY STOP IN YOUR MANEUVERS AGAINST *HIM* IN ALL FACETS, THOUGHTS, AND THE MAKING OF GODLY DECISIONS. I LOOSE THE WISDOM, KNOWLEDGE AND UNDERSTANDING OF GOD'S WORD TO FILL *HIS* MIND; AND WITH CONFIDENCE *HE* WILL MAKE GOOD DECISIONS ACCORDING TO THE LEADING OF THE HOLY SPIRIT."

"FATHER, I thank YOU that the communication of my faith through intercession becomes effectual by acknowledging every good thing which is in the spirit man of _____ in CHRIST

JESUS. *He* hears the voice of the Good Shepherd. *He* also hears YOUR Voice, FATHER, and the voice of a stranger *he* will NOT follow."

"FATHER, _____ believes in *his* heart and says with *his* mouth that this Day, "**The Will of GOD is done in *my* life**." *He* walks in a manner worthy of YOU LORD, fully pleasing to YOU and desiring to please YOU in all things, bearing fruit in every good work and making good decisions. JESUS has been made unto *him* wisdom. *He* single-mindedly walks in YOUR Wisdom expecting to know what to do in every situation through the HOLY SPIRIT and is on top of every circumstance!"

"_____ rolls all *his* works upon YOU, LORD, and YOU make *his* thoughts agreeable to YOUR Will, and so *his* plans are established and succeed. YOU direct *his* steps and make them sure. *He* understands and firmly grasps what the Will of the LORD is for *his* life, which is not vague, thoughtless, or foolish. *He* stands firm and mature in spiritual growth convinced and fully assured in everything Willed by GOD."

"FATHER, YOU have appointed _____ to progressively come to know YOUR Will–that is to perceive, to recognize more strongly and clearly, and to become better and more intimately acquainted with YOUR Will. *He* thanks YOU, FATHER, for the HOLY SPIRIT, Who abides permanently in *him* and Who guides *him* into all truth – the whole truth with insight–and speaks whatever the HOLY SPIRIT hears from the FATHER and announces and declares to *him* the things that are to come. *He* has the mind of CHRIST, Who holds the thoughts, feelings, and purposes of *His* heart."

"So, FATHER, _____ has entered into YOUR blessed rest by adhering, trusting, and relying on YOU, in the Name of JESUS; the intercessors call this to be accomplished. As intercessors, we thank YOU continually that this prayer of agreement from our hearts through faith is DONE! Hallelujah, Praise the LORD! Amen!"

## SCRIPTURE REFERENCE:

| | | |
|---|---|---|
| Proverbs 9:10 | Philemon 6 | Colossians 4:12 |
| John 10:27, 5 | Acts 22:14 | Colossians 1:9-10 |
| I John 2:20, 27 | I Corinthians 1:30 | I Corinthians 2:16 |
| James 1:5-8 | Hebrews 4:10 | Proverbs 16:3, 9 |
| John 16:13 | Ephesians 5:17 | |

# To Walk in Love

"FATHER, in JESUS Name, thank YOU that the Love of GOD has been shed abroad, poured forth into my heart by the HOLY SPIRIT, Who has been given to me. I keep and treasure YOUR Word. The love for the FATHER has been perfected and completed in me, and perfect love casts and drives out all fear.

FATHER, I am your child, and **I am committed to walk in the GOD Perfect Love.** I endured long-suffering, I am patient, and I am kind. I am never envious and never boil over with jealousy. I am not boastful or vainglorious; I do not display myself as being haughtily. I am not rude or unmannerly and I do not act unbecomingly. I do not insist on my own rights or my own way for I am not self-seeking, touchy, fretful, or resentful. I take no account of any evil done to me and pay no attention when I have been suffered wrongly. I do not rejoice at injustice and unrighteousness, but I rejoice when GOD'S justice and truth prevails. I bear up under anything and everything that comes. I am ever ready to believe the best of others. My hopes are fadeless under all circumstances. I endure everything without weakening, for YOUR Love has never failed me.

FATHER, I *bless* and *pray* for those who persecute me with a forgiving heart toward those who are cruel in their attitude toward me. I bless them and do not curse them. Therefore, my love abounds yet more and more in YOUR Knowledge and in all Judgment. I approve things that are excellent. I am sincere and without offense till the Day of

CHRIST. I am filled with the faith of Righteousness and the fruits of the SPIRIT.

Everywhere I go I commit to plant seeds of love. FATHER, I thank YOU for preparing hearts ahead of time to receive this love. I know that the seeds of faith will produce YOUR Love in their hearts which you have dealt with and have revealed their unjust ways.

FATHER, I thank YOU that as I flow in YOUR love and wisdom, people are being blessed by my life. FATHER, YOU make me to find favor, compassion, and loving-kindness with others.

I am rooted deep in love and I am securely founded in love knowing that YOU are on my side, and nothing is able to separate me from YOUR Love, which is in CHRIST JESUS my LORD. Thank YOU, FATHER, in JESUS precious Name. Amen!"

## SCRIPTURE REFERENCES:

| | | |
|---|---|---|
| Romans 5:5 | Philippians 1:9-11 | I John 2:5 |
| John 13:34 | I John 4:18 | I Corinthians 3:6 |
| I Corinthians 13:4-8 | Daniel 1:9 | Romans 12:14 |
| Ephesians 3:17 | Matthew 5:44 | Romans 8: 31, 39 |

# To Watch What You Say

"FATHER, today, I make a commitment to YOU in the Name of JESUS. I turn from idle words and foolishly talk that is contrary to my true desire of myself and toward others. YOUR Word says that the tongue defiles; that the tongue sets on fire the course of nature; that the tongue is set on fire from hell, for it is untamed and can bring forth much harm to others. In the Name of JESUS, I called the HOLY SPIRIT to help me become mindful of the things I am about to speak, so my tongue will prove you can do the impossible even in taming one's tongue that can hurt or heal and encourage others.

**In the Name of JESUS, I am determined to take control of my tongue.** I am determined that hell will not set my tongue on fire. I renounce, reject, and repent of every word that has ever proceeded out of my mouth against YOU GOD and YOUR Operation. I cancel its power by dedicating my mouth to speak excellent and princely things and the opening of my lips for right things. My mouth will only speak truth.

I am the Righteousness of GOD; I set the course of my life for abundance, for wisdom, for health, and for joy. Everything I speak is pleasing to GOD. I refuse to compromise or err from pure and sound words. The words of my mouth and my deeds will show forth YOUR Righteousness and YOUR Salvation all of my days. I guard my heart and my mouth with all diligence. I refuse to give Satan any place in me. I am determined no longer to be double minded by the words that may come from my mouth.

FATHER, YOUR Words take first place to me. They are Spirit and Life. I let the Word dwell in me richly in all Wisdom. The ability of GOD is released within me by the words of my mouth and by the Word of GOD. I speak YOUR Words out of my mouth. They are alive in me. YOU are alive and working in me. So, I can boldly say that my words are words of faith, words of Power, words of Love, and words of Life. They produce good things in my life and in the lives of others. Because I choose YOUR Words for my lips, I choose YOUR Will for my life, and I go forth in the power of those words to perform them in JESUS' Name."

## SCRIPTURE REFERENCES:

| | | |
|---|---|---|
| Ephesians 5:4 | II Timothy 2:16 | James 3:6 |
| Proverbs 8:6-7 | II Corinthians 5:21 | Proverbs 4:23 |
| Proverbs 21:23 | Ephesians 4:27 | James 1:6 |
| John 6:63 | Colossians 3:16 | Philemon 6 |

# To Live Free from Worry

"FATHER, I thank YOU that I have been delivered from the power of darkness and translated into the Kingdom of YOUR Dear SON. **I commit to live free from worry in the Name of JESUS** for the Law of the Spirit of Life in CHRIST JESUS has made me *free* from the law of sin and death.

I humble myself under YOUR Mighty Hand that in due time YOU may exalt me casting all my cares (*name them*)—all my anxieties, all my worries, all my concerns, once and for all—on YOU; for YOU affectionately care for me and watch over me carefully. YOU consistently sustain me and will never allow YOUR Righteousness to be moved—made to slip, fall, or fail me!

FATHER, I delight myself in YOU, for YOUR perfection engulfs me in YOUR Ways.

I cast down every imagination (reasoning), and every high thing that exalts itself against the Knowledge of YOU, and bring into captivity every thought to the obedience of CHRIST. I lay aside every weight, and the sin of worry that attempts to pull me down. I run with patience the race that is set before me, looking unto JESUS, the Author and Finisher of my faith.

FATHER, I thank YOU, for YOU have been able to keep that which I have committed unto you. I think on (fix my mind on) those things that are true, honest, just, pure, lovely, of good report, virtuous, and deserving of praise. I do not allow my heart to be troubled. I abide in YOUR Words, and YOUR Words abide in me. Therefore, FATHER, I will **not** forget who I am in YOU. I look into the Perfect Law of Liberty and continue therein, being not a forgetful hearer, *but a doer of the Word* and therefore blessed by responding in my works of faith in doing well.

Thank YOU, FATHER. *I am carefree.* I walk in that peace which passes all understanding in JESUS' Name!"

## SCRIPTURE REFERENCES:

| | | |
|---|---|---|
| Colossians 1:13 | Romans 8:2 | I Peter 5:6-7 |
| Psalm 55:22 | Psalm 37:4-5 | Psalm 138:8 |
| II Corinthians 10:5 | Hebrews 12:1-2 | II Timothy 1:12 |
| Philippians 4:8 | John 14:1 | John 15:7 |
| James 1:22-25 | Philippians 4:6 | |

# From Corrupt Companions

"SATAN, IN JESUS' NAME, TAKE YOUR HANDS OFF _____ _____. I BIND YOU FROM *HIS* LIFE. YOU STOP YOUR MANEUVERS AGAINST *HIM*. I LOOSE GOD'S POWERFUL WORD OF PROTECTION OVER _____ SO *HE* CAN BE SET FREE IN THE NAME JESUS."

"FATHER, I thank YOU for delivering _____ from corrupt and depraved people. I confess that _____ has awakened and returned to a sober sense and his right mind and sins no more. _____, who separates himself from contact with contaminating influences and cleanses himself from everything that would defile his spirit, mind and body.

_____ lives and conducts himself honorably and becomingly as in the open light of day; not in reveling (carousing) and drunkenness, not in immorality and dishonesty (sensuality and licentiousness), not in quarreling and jealousy. _____ is done with every trace of wickedness (depravity, malignity) and all deceit and insincerity (pretense, hypocrisy), grudges, slander and evil speaking of every kind.

_____ is loyally subject (submissive) to the governing (civil) authorities—not resisting nor setting himself up against them. _____ is obedient, prepared and willing to do any upright and honorable work. _____ walks as a companion with wise men, so he will also be wise.

_____ sins have been forgiven. _____ is pardoned through the Name of JESUS, because he has confessed sins to the LORD JESUS. _____ is victorious over the wicked one because he has come to know and recognize and is aware of the FATHER'S Will. The Word dwells and remains in hm, and he dwells in the SON and in the FATHER at all times. GOD'S Nature abides in him—HIS principle of Life, the Divine Spirit, remains permanently within him and he cannot practice sinning because _____ is born of the Spirit of GOD. The Law of the Spirit of Life in CHRIST JESUS has made him free from the law of sin and death. Thank YOU, FATHER, that the HOLY SPIRIT is watching over and teaching me as a new child rejoicing in YOUR Word. He rejoices that the Word is being perfected in him, in JESUS' Name!"

## SCRIPTURE REFERENCES:

| | | |
|---|---|---|
| I Corinthians 15:33-34a | | II Timothy 2:21 |
| | II Corinthians 7:1 | |
| Romans 13:13 | I Peter 2:1 | Romans 13:1-2 |
| Titus 3:1 | Proverbs 13:20 | Proverbs 28:7 |
| I Thessalonians 5:22 | I John 2:12-16 | I John 2:21, 24 |
| I John 3:9 | Romans 8:2 | Jeremiah 1:12 |

# From Satan and His Demonic Forces Regarding:

## (Alcoholism, Gambling, Narcotics, the Occults, etc.)

*If the person that you are interceding has not confessed JESUS as their LORD and SAVIOR, pray specifically that the HOLY SPIRIT to forever be in their midst until they call upon the LORD for their salvation. Stand-fast to your confess of faith and thank the FATHER that it is done in the Name of JESUS. Then pray the following:*

"FATHER, in the Name of JESUS, I come boldly to YOUR Throne of Grace and present _____ before YOU. I stand in the gap and intercede on behalf of _____ knowing that the HOLY SPIRIT within me and the angels round about him, strengthening him in faith and the prayer of thanksgiving against the evils that would attempt to hold _____ in bondage. I unwrap _____ from the bonds of wickedness through the power of prayer; I take the Shield of Faith to quench every fiery dart of the adversary that would come against _____.

FATHER, YOU said, whatever I bind on earth is bound in Heaven and whatever I loose on earth is loosened in Heaven. YOU said for me to cast out demons, in the Name of JESUS.

"SO I SPEAK TO YOU, SATAN, AND TO THE PRINCIPALITIES, THE POWERS, THE RULERS OF THE DARKNESS, AND SPIRITUAL WICKEDNESS IN HIGH PLACES AND THE DEMONIC SPIRITS OF (*name of spirits*) ASSIGNED TO _____. I TAKE AUTHORITY OVER YOU AND BIND YOU AWAY FROM _____ IN THE MIGHTY NAME OF JESUS. YOU LOOSE _____ AND LET HIM GO FREE, IN THE NAME OF JESUS. I DEMAND THAT YOU STOP YOUR MANEUVERS NOW. SATAN, YOUR WORKS ARE SPOILED AND YOU ARE A DEFEATED ENEMY."

I call forth ministering Spirits of GOD, YOUR angels, to go forth in the Name of JESUS and provide the necessary help to assist and strength for _____.

FATHER, I have laid hold of _____ salvation and his confession of the LORDSHIP of JESUS CHRIST. I speak of these things that are not as though they were; for I choose to look at the unseen—the Eternal things of GOD. I say that Satan will not take advantage of _____: for I am not ignorant of Satan's devices. I resist Satan and he has run in terror from _____, in the Name of JESUS. For the Word of GOD says, that Satan may come toward you one way, but GOD will force him to flee seven ways. I give Satan no place in _____. I plead the Blood of the LAMB over _____ for Satan and his cohorts have no authority over _____ and he is an overcomer by the Blood of JESUS and YOUR Word. FATHER, I thank YOU that I have authority and power to tread on serpents and scorpions and over all the power of the enemy in behalf of _____. _____ is delivered from this present evil world. He is delivered from the powers of darkness and translated into the Kingdom of YOUR Dear SON!

FATHER, I ask YOU now to fill those vacant places within _____ through YOUR redemptive and powerful Word, the HOLY SPIRIT, YOUR Love, YOUR Wisdom, YOUR Righteousness, and YOUR Revelation Knowledge, in the Name of JESUS.

I thank YOU, FATHER, that _____ is redeemed by the Blood of JESUS and taken out of the hand of Satan. He is justified and made righteous by the Blood of JESUS and belongs to YOU—spirit, soul and body. I thank YOU that every enslaving bondage is broken from _____ and he will no longer be a slave of anything or be brought under its power, in the Name of JESUS. _____ has escaped the snare of the devil that has held him captive and from this point forward _____ desires to do YOUR Will, FATHER, which is to Glorify YOU in his spirit, mind and body.

Thank YOU, FATHER, that JESUS was manifested in the destructive works of the devil. Satan's works are destroyed in _____'s life in the Name of JESUS. Hallelujah! _____ walks in the Kingdom of GOD which is Righteousness, Peace, and Joy in the HOLY SPIRIT! Praise the LORD!"

*Once this prayer has been prayed, thank the FATHER that Satan and his cohorts are bound. Stand firm, fixed, immovable, and steadfast on your confessions of faith (refuse the things you see or hear) as you intercede on this person's behalf for* **"greater is HE that is in you, than he who is in the world."** (I John 4:4).

## SCRIPTURE REFERENCES:

| | | |
|---|---|---|
| Hebrews 4:16 | Ezekiel 22:30 | Romans 8:26 |
| Isaiah 58:6 | Ephesians 6:16 | Matthew 18:18 |
| Mark 16:17 | Ephesians 6:12 | Colossians 2:15 |
| Matthew 12:29 | Hebrews 1:14 | Romans 4:17 |
| II Corinthians 4:18 | II Corinthians 2:11 | James 4:7 |
| Ephesians 4:27 | Revelation 12:11 | Luke 10:19 |
| Galatians 1:4 | Colossians 1:13 | Matthew 12:43-45 |
| I Corinthians 6:12 | II Timothy 2:26 | I John 3:8 |
| | Romans 14:17 | |

# **Deliverance of Loved Ones from Cults**

"FATHER, in the Name of JESUS, we come before YOU in prayer and in faith believing that YOUR Word runs swiftly throughout the earth for the Word of GOD is not chained or imprisoned. We bring before YOU _____ (*those and families of those involved in cults*). FATHER, stretch forth YOUR Hand from above, rescue and deliver _____ out of great waters, from the land of hostile aliens whose mouth speaks deceit and whose right hand is raised in taking a fraudulent oath. Their mouths must be stopped for they are mentally distressing and subverting _____ and whole families by teaching what they should not be taught, for the purpose of getting base advantage and disreputable gain. But praise GOD, they will not get very far for their rash folly will become obvious to everybody!

Execute justice, precious FATHER, from the spirit of the oppressed. Set the prisoners free, open the eyes of the blind, lift up the bowed down, heal the brokenhearted, bind up their wounds curing their pains and sorrow. Lift up the humble and down-trodden and cast the wicked down to the ground in the Mighty Name of JESUS.

Turn back the hearts of the disobedient, incredulous, and unpersuadable to the Wisdom of the Upright, the Knowledge, and Holy Love of the Will of GOD in order to make ready for YOU, LORD; a people perfectly prepared in spirit, adjusted, disposed, and placed in the right moral state.

FATHER, YOU said in YOUR Word to refrain our voice from weeping and our eyes from tears for our prayers will be rewarded and _____ will return from the enemy's land and come again to their own country. You will save our offspring from the land of their exile, from the east and the west — sons from afar and daughters from the ends of the earth. We will see _____ walking in the ways of piety and virtue revering YOUR Name, FATHER. Those who err in spirit will come to understanding. Those who murmur discontentedly will accept instruction in YOUR Ways. FATHER, YOU contend with those who contend with us and YOU bring forth safety to _____ and ease him."

"SATAN, WE SPEAK TO YOU, IN THE NAME OF JESUS. WE BIND YOU, THE PRINCIPALITIES, THE POWERS, THE RULERS OF THE DARKNESS, AND THE WICKED SPIRITS IN HEAVENLY PLACES, AND WE TEAR DOWN STRONGHOLDS USING THE MIGHTY WEAPONS GOD HAS PROVIDED FOR US IN THE NAME OF JESUS. WE SPEAK TO GREED, SELFISHNESS, PRIDE, ARROGANCE, BOASTFULNESS, ABUSE, BLASPHEMY, DISOBEDIENCE, UNGRATEFULNESS, PROFANITY, REBELLION, PERVERSENESS, SLANDER, IMMORALITY, FEROCITY, HATRED, TREACHERY, CONCEIT, LUST, MATERIALISM, ERROR, DECEIT, SPIRIT OF ANTICHRIST, UNWORTHINESS, FILTHINESS, CRUELTY, HOSTILITY, DEPRAVITY, DISTORTION, UNGODLINESS, AND FALSITY AND LOOSE YOU FROM ALL DIABOLICAL ASSIGNMENTS AGAINST _____. WE CANCEL ALL NEGATIVE

TALKING, DOUBT AND UNBELIEF. SATAN WILL NOT USE THIS AGAINST _____. THEREFORE, WE LOOSE GOD'S PERFECT UNCONDITIONAL LOVE, WISDOM, KNOWLEDGE AND UNDERSTANDING FOR _____ TO SEE THE DIFFERENCE BETWEEN THE TWO WITH TOTAL UNDERSTANDING, KNOWING THEY ARE MAKING THE RIGHT DECISION NOT TO FOLLOW THE ENEMY, BUT TO PUT GOD FIRST AND FOREMOST IN THEIR LIFE, IN JESUS NAME."

"We commission the ministering spirits to go forth and dispel these forces of darkness and bring _____ home, in the Name of JESUS.

FATHER, we believe and confess that _____ has had knowledge of and has been acquainted with the Word which was able to instruct and give _____ the understanding for Salvation which comes through faith in CHRIST JESUS. LORD, we pray and believe that YOU certainly will deliver _____ and draw _____ to YOURSELF from every assault of evil and preserve and bring _____ safely into YOUR Heavenly Kingdom. Glory to YOU, FATHER, Who delivers those for whom we intercede, in JESUS' Name!

*Once this prayer has been prayed for an individual, confess it as done. Thank the FATHER that deliverance is theirs as they return from the enemy's land. Thank GOD that Satan is bound. Thank GOD for their salvation.*

## SCRIPTURE REFERENCES:

| | | |
|---|---|---|
| Psalm 147:15 | II Timothy 2:9 | Psalm 144:7-8 |
| Titus 1:11 | II Timothy 3:9 | Psalm 146:7-8 |
| Psalm 147:3-6 | Luke 1:17 | Jeremiah 31:16-17 |
| Jeremiah 46:27 | Isaiah 43:5-6 | Isaiah 29:23-24 |
| Isaiah 49:25 | Matthew 18:18 | II Timothy 3:2-9 |
| Hebrews 1:14 | II Timothy 3:15 | II Timothy 4:18 |
| | Job 22:30 | |

# From Bad Habits

"FATHER, by faith in the Name of JESUS and according to YOUR Word, I hereby believe in my heart and say with my mouth that JESUS is the LORD of _____'s life. I also confess that from this day forward _____ is set free and delivered from the habit(s) of _____ in the Name of JESUS."

"SATAN YOU AND ALL YOUR PRINCIPALITIES, POWERS, AND MASTER SPIRITS WHO RULE THE DARKNESS, AND SPIRITUAL WICKEDNESS IN HIGH PLACES ARE BOUND UP AND _____ IS LOOSED FROM YOU, IN THE NAME OF JESUS, AS IT IS WRITTEN IN MATTHEW 18:18-19. NO LONGER CAN YOU, SATAN, HARASS OR OPERATE ANY OF YOUR UNCLEAN SPIRITS OR HABITS OVER _____, HE WILL NOT BECOME THE SLAVE OF ANYTHING THAT EXALTS ITSELF OVER THE WORD OF GOD OR BE BROUGHT UNDER ITS POWER."

"I hereby confess that _____ is strengthened and reinforced with mighty power in his inner being by the HOLY SPIRIT that lives and dwells in his heart and mind. _____ is strong in the LORD. He is empowered through his union with the LORD. He draws strength from the LORD...that Strength which HIS boundless might is provided for _____.

_____ arms himself with the Full Armor of GOD, that is Armor for a heavily armed soldier which GOD has supplied for him….the Helmet of Salvation...loins girded with Truth...breastplate of Righteousness...his feet shod with the preparation of the Gospel of Peace…his Shield of Faith…and the Sword of the Spirit, which is the Word of GOD. With GOD'S Armor on, he is able to stand up against all the strategies, deceits, and fiery darts of Satan, in the Name of JESUS.

As an act of our faith, _____'s will is to walk and talk the Words of faith, he receives complete strength from the LORD and the LORD puts before him total freedom NOW. He is set free and delivered because he has called upon the Name of the LORD according to that which is written in YOUR Word.

_____ has self-discipline within his body and mind subduing the enemy to be under his feet. He is strong. He is free. He withstands temptation because JESUS is the LORD of his life. JESUS is his High Priest and with JESUS and the FATHER being at his sides, he is made to be strengthened for all things...because greater is HE Who is in him than, he who is in the world.

Thank YOU, LORD. I praise YOU that _____ is whole and redeemed from every evil work. With YOU and YOUR Word being in control of his body and his flesh. It does not nor can it ever again control him anymore, in the Name of JESUS. Hallelujah!"

## SCRIPTURE REFERENCES:

Romans 10:9-10, 13  Matthew 18:18-19  I Corinthians 6:12
II Corinthians 10:4-5  Ephesians 3:16  Ephesians 6:10-17
Hebrews 4:14-16  I John 4:4  Romans 8:4, 9
Romans 12:21  Romans 13:14

# From Depression

"FATHER, YOU are my refuge and my high tower and my stronghold in times of trouble for YOU have given to me a sound mind. I lean on and confidently putting my trust in YOU; for YOU have not forsaken me because I seek YOU for the Authority of YOUR Word and the right of its necessity. I praise YOU because YOU are the help of my Countenance and my GOD.

LORD, YOU lift up those who are bowed down. Therefore, I am strong and my heart takes courage. I establish myself on righteousness—right, in conformity with YOUR Will and Order. I am far even from the thought of oppression or destruction, for I dwell in GOD'S Perfect Love through JESUS; therefore, I have been set free from all fear and from any form of terror, for it will not come near me.

FATHER, YOU have perfect thoughts and plans for my welfare and peace *for my mind is stayed steadfast in YOU*. I stop allowing myself to be agitated, disturbed, intimidated, cowardly and unsettled."

"SATAN, I RESIST YOU AND EVERY OPPRESSIVE SPIRIT, IN THE NAME OF JESUS. I RESIST THE SPIRITS OF FEAR, DISCOURAGEMENT, SELF-PITY, AND DEPRESSION. I SPEAK THE WORD OF TRUTH, IN THE POWER OF GOD, AND SATAN, I GIVE YOU NO PLACE; I GIVE NO OPPORTUNITY TO YOU. I AM DELIVERED, FOR I HAVE LOOSENED YOU FROM OPPRESSION BY THE BLOOD OF THE LAMB."

FATHER, I thank YOU that I have been given a Spirit of Power and of Love and of a Calm and Sound mind and disciplined with Self-control. I have the mind of CHRIST and hold the thoughts, feelings, and purposes of HIS Heart. I have a fresh, renewed mental and spiritual attitude for I am constantly being renewed in the spirit within my mind being supported by YOUR Word, through the HOLY SPIRIT working mightily within me.

Therefore, I am embraced, reinvigorated, cut through, made to be firm and assured with understanding; a smooth and straight path for my feet—safe, upright, and having a happy path that brings healing causing me to make good decisions and to go in the right direction. I arise from the depression and prostration in which circumstances have attempted to keep me down. I rise to new life. I shine and am radiant with the Glory of the LORD.

Thank YOU, FATHER, in JESUS' Name, that I am set free from every evil work. I praise YOU that the Joy of the LORD is my strength and stronghold! Hallelujah!"

## SCRIPTURE REFERENCES:

| | | |
|---|---|---|
| Psalm 9:9-10 | Psalm 42:5, 11 | Psalm 146:8 |
| Psalm 31:22-24 | Isaiah 35:3-4 | Isaiah 54:14 |
| Isaiah 50:10 | Jeremiah 29:11-13 | Isaiah 26:3 |
| John 14:27 | James 4:7 | Ephesians 4:27 |
| Luke 4:18-19 | II Timothy 1:7 | I Corinthians 2:16 |
| Philippians 2:5 | Ephesians 4:23-24 | Hebrews 12:12-13 |
| Isaiah 60:1 | Galatians 1:4 | Nehemiah 8:10 |

# To Receive JESUS as SAVIOR and LORD

"FATHER, it is written in YOUR Word, that if I repent of my sins and confess with my mouth that JESUS is my LORD, and believe in my heart that YOU rose from the dead, I will be saved. Therefore, FATHER, I confess that JESUS is my LORD. I make HIM LORD of my life right now. FATHER, I believe in my heart that YOU raised JESUS from the dead. I renounce my past life with Satan.

I thank YOU for forgiving me of all my sins. JESUS is my LORD, and I am a new creation. Old things have passed away; my shoulders are weightless. From this day forward, all things will become new; for I have a renewed spirit and even my outward person will daily grow into new ways in CHRIST JESUS, in JESUS' Name. Amen."

*(It is important to share with others your new declaration and that JESUS is your LORD.)*

## SCRIPTURE REFERENCES:

| | | |
|---|---|---|
| John 3:16 | John 6:37 | John 10:10b |
| Romans 3:23 | II Corinthians 5:19 | John 16:8-9 |
| Romans 5:8 | John 14:6 | Romans 10:9-10 |
| Romans 10:13 | Ephesians 2:1-10 | II Corinthians 5:17 |
| John 1:12 | II Corinthians 5:21 | |

# For Salvation in General

"FATHER, it is written in YOUR Word, *First of all, and then I admonish and urge that petitions, prayers, intercessions and thanksgivings be offered on behalf of all men!* (I Timothy 2:1)

Therefore, FATHER, as we bring forth those who are lost in the knowledge of knowing JESUS as their LORD and SAVIOR; through the Power of intercession prayer before you throughout this world, allow GOD'S Perfect Love, through the HOLY SPIRIT, to begin to convince every man, woman, and child, from the farthest corners of the earth, to desire to come before YOU. As we intercede, we use our faith believing that thousands this day have the opportunity to make JESUS as their LORD.

"FOR EVERYONE WHO HAS THIS OPPORTUNITY, SATAN, WE BIND YOUR BLINDING SPIRIT OF ANTICHRIST AND LOOSE YOU FROM YOUR ASSIGNMENT AGAINST THOSE WHO HAVE THAT OPPORTUNITY TO MAKE JESUS LORD OF THEIR LIVES."

"We ask the LORD of the Harvest to graciously put the perfect laborer to cross their paths in this life and prepare them who will have ears to hear the Good News of the Gospel as it is shared in a special way so that they will listen and understand it. We believe that they will not be able to resist the wooing of the HOLY SPIRIT for YOU, FATHER, reveal to them through the Light of JESUS, to see their whole life and allow them to see through YOUR Light that shines so Bright, they see their need to repentance by YOUR goodness and love.

We confess that they will see JESUS, Who they may have never heard of has being made the way for them to have Salvation by the confessing of their sins and making JESUS to be LORD of their lives. They will have understanding of the ONE, Who they have never heard of, and HIS Name is JESUS. The Revelation of the HOLY SPIRIT will show them that they can be freed of the snare of the devil that has held them captive. They will open their eyes and turn from darkness to Light—from the power of Satan to YOU, GOD!"

## SCRIPTURE REFERENCES:
I Timothy 2:1-2      Romans 2:4        Job 22:30
Romans 15:21         Matthew 18:18     II Timothy 2:26

## For Specific Salvation

"FATHER, in the Name of JESUS, we come before YOU in prayer and in faith, believing. It is written in YOUR Word that JESUS came to save the lost. YOU wish for all men to be saved and to know YOUR Divine Truth. Therefore, FATHER, we bring _____ before YOU this day."

"SATAN, WE BIND YOU, IN THE NAME OF JESUS, AND LOOSE YOU FROM THE ACTIVITIES IN _____'S LIFE!"

"FATHER, we ask the LORD of the Harvest to thrust the perfect person into *his* path, a person to share YOUR Gospel in a special way so that *he* will hear and listen with understanding to the Voice of the HOLY SPIRIT. As YOUR laborer ministers to *him*, we believe that he will come to *his* senses…come out of the gripe of the enemy that has imprisoned *him* and to choose to become a Child of GOD, in JESUS Name we declare that *he* will make JESUS to be LORD of his life.

Your Word says that YOU will deliver those for whom we intercede, who are not innocent, through the cleanness of their hands made capable through JESUS. We're standing on YOUR Word and from this moment on, FATHER, we will praise YOU and thank YOU for *his* salvation. We have committed this matter into YOUR Hands and with our faith as we see with spiritual eyes that _____ is saved, filled with YOUR Spirit, with a full and clear knowledge of YOUR Word. Amen — *So be it!*"

*Each day, thank the LORD for this person's salvation. Rejoice and praise GOD for the victory! Confess the above prayer as done! Thank HIM for sending the right laborer. Thank HIM that Satan is bound. Hallelujah!*

## SCRIPTURE REFERENCES:

| | | |
|---|---|---|
| Luke 19:10 | II Timothy 2:26 | Matthew 18:18 |
| Job 22:30 | Matthew 9:38 | |

# To Receive the Infilling of the HOLY SPIRIT

"My Heavenly FATHER, I am YOUR child, for I believe in my heart that JESUS has been raised from the dead, I believe that HE has breathed upon me the HOLY SPIRIT since I have confessed JESUS as my LORD.

JESUS said, *How much more will your Heavenly FATHER give the HOLY SPIRIT to those that ask HIM.* I ask YOU now, in the Name of JESUS, to fill me with the HOLY SPIRIT. I step into the fullness and power that I desire, in the Name of JESUS. I confess that I am a Spirit-filled Christian. As I yield my vocal organs, I desire to speak and sing in YOUR Heavenly Language as the HOLY SPIRIT gives me utterance within my spirit so I also will begin to speak with what HE have given to me; I will speak those words just as a baby begins to speak words that they don't understand, in the Name of JESUS. I praise YOU LORD!"

## SCRIPTURE REFERENCES:

| | | |
|---|---|---|
| John 14:16-17 | Acts 10:44-46 | Luke 11:13 |
| Acts 19:2, 5, 6 | Acts 1:8a | I Corinthians 14:2-15 |
| Acts 2:4 39 | I Corinthians 14:18, 27 | Acts 2:32-33, |
| Ephesians 6:18 | Acts 8:12-17 | Jude 1:20 |

# A Confession of Forgiveness for the Believer

"FATHER, in the Name of JESUS, I make a fresh commitment to YOU to live in peace and harmony, not only with the other brothers and sisters of the Body of CHRIST, but also with my friends, associates, neighbors and family. I desire to walk in YOUR Love that cast or drives out all fear and through JESUS SPIRIT living within me, I will shine bright with the LIGHT of HIS Glory.

I will let go of all bitterness, resentment, envying, strife and unkindness in any form. I give no place to the devil, in JESUS' Name. Now FATHER, I ask for YOUR forgiveness and that YOU would give me a forgiving heart toward those who I may have hurt and they may have hurt me in any way. By faith, I receive it, having assurance that I am cleansed from all unrighteousness through JESUS CHRIST. I ask YOU to forgive and release all who I have wronged and those who have hurt me. I forgive and release them. Deal with me, so I can show them the beauty of Your Mercy and Lovingkindness.

From this moment on, I purpose to walk in love, to seek peace, to live in agreement, and to conduct myself toward others in a manner that is pleasing to YOU. I know that I am in right standing with YOU and YOUR ears are attentive to my prayers, and in the same manner that my ears will be quick to hear YOUR Voice.

It is written in YOUR Word that the Love of GOD has been shed abroad, poured forth into my heart by the HOLY SPIRIT, Who has been given to me. I believe that YOUR Perfect Love flows forth into the lives of everyone I know so I may be filled to overflow with love and abound in the fruits of the SPIRIT with Righteousness which brings Glory and Honor unto YOU, FATHER, in JESUS' Name. So be it!"

## SCRIPTURE REFERENCES:

| | | |
|---|---|---|
| Romans 12:16-18, 10 | Philippians 2:2 | Ephesians 4:31, 27 |
| I John 1:9 | Mark 11:25 | Ephesians 4:32 |
| I Peter 3:8, 11-12 | Colossians 1:10 | Romans 5:5 |
| | Philippians 1:9, 11 | |

# Renewed Fellowship

"FATHER, YOU hasten YOUR Word to perform it. I believe and confess that _____ is a disciple of CHRIST, taught of YOU, learning to be obedient to YOUR Will. Great is his peace and undisturbed composure. _____ has YOU in Person for his Teacher. He has listened and learned from YOU and has come to know the Love of JESUS.

_____ continues to hold to the things he has learned and of which he is convinced by the HOLY SPIRIT. From childhood he has had knowledge of and been acquainted with the Word which is able to instruct him and give him the understanding of the Salvation which comes through faith in CHRIST JESUS. FATHER, YOU will heal _____, lead _____, and bring recompense and restore comfort to _____.

JESUS gives _____ Eternal Life. He will never lose it or perish throughout the ages, to all eternity. _____'s spiritual experience will never by any means be destroyed. No one is able to snatch _____ out of FATHER'S Hand. YOU, FATHER, have given _____ to JESUS. YOU are greater and mightier in him that than the enemy is in this world. _____ will walk according to YOUR Principles and Standards and in YOUR Ways."

"IN THE NAME OF JESUS, SATAN AND EVERY HINDERING SPIRIT, YOU ARE BOUND FROM_____'S LIFE. HE HAS BEEN LOOSENED AND SET FREE TO LIVE IN THE PRESENCE OF THE LORD GOD, IN JESUS NAME."

_____ has come into the fellowship with CHRIST, the MESSIAH, and shares in all HE has for him as he holds his first renewed confidence and original assured expectation firm and unshaken to the end. _____ does not cast away his confidence for it has great recompense of reward.

Thank YOU for giving _____ by giving him YOUR Wisdom and Revelation Knowledge, — quickening him by YOUR Word. Thank YOU that _____ enjoys his fellowship with YOU and JESUS as well as the fellowship with other believers."

## SCRIPTURE REFERENCES:

| | | |
|---|---|---|
| Jeremiah 1:12 | John 6:45 | Isaiah 54:13 |
| II Timothy 3:14-15 | Isaiah 57:18 | John 10:28-29 |
| I John 5:16 | II Timothy 2:26 | I Corinthians 11:31 |
| Matthew 18:18 | Hebrews 3:14 | Hebrews 10:35 |
| Ephesians 1:17 | I John 1:3 | |

# For Boldness and Authority

"FATHER, in the Name of JESUS, I am of good courage. I pray YOU grant to me abound with all **boldness** as I speak forth YOUR Word. I pray that I have freedom in YOUR Word and the **Authority** YOU have given to me so when I open my mouth to proclaim **boldly** the mystery of the Good News of the Gospel—that I may declare it **boldly** as I ought to do.

FATHER, I believe I received that **boldness** now, in the Name of JESUS. Therefore, I have **boldness** to enter into the HOLY of HOLIES by the Blood of JESUS. Because of my faith in HIM, I dare to have the **boldness and authority** (*courage and confidence*) of free access—an unreserved approach to YOU with freedom and without fear. I humbly and fearlessly draw near YOU with confidently and **boldly** approach the Throne of YOUR Grace as I receive mercy and find grace to help in good times for every need. I am **bold** to pray. I come before the Throne of GOD with my petitions, and for others who do not know how to ascend to the Throne through the Power of Prayer.

I will be **bold** toward Satan, his demons, evil spirits, sickness, disease, and poverty; for JESUS is the Head of all rulers and authority—of every angelic principalities and power. Disarming them who were enraged against me, HE (JESUS) made a **bold display** and public example of them triumphing over them. I am **bold** to say, 'Satan, you are a defeated foe, for my GOD and JESUS as my LORD reigns above all things!'

I take comfort and am encouraged with confidence and *boldly* say, 'The LORD is my Helper, I will not be seized with alarm—I will not fear or dread or be terrified. What can man do to me?' I dare to proclaim the Word toward Heaven, toward hell, and within this world around me.

I am *bold* and walk with *authority* as a lion for I have been made the Righteousness unto GOD, in CHRIST JESUS. I am complete in HIM! Praise the Name of JESUS!"

## SCRIPTURE REFERENCES:

| | | |
|---|---|---|
| Psalm 27:14 | Acts 4:29 | Ephesians 6:19-20 |
| Mark 11:23-24 | Hebrews 10:19 | Ephesians 3:12 |
| Hebrews 4:16 | Colossians 2:10, 15 | Hebrews 13:6 |
| Proverbs 28:1 | II Corinthians 5:21 | |

# On Improving Communication with a Loved One

"_____ is a disciple of CHRIST—taught of the LORD and obedient to HIS Will. Great is the peace and undisturbed composure within him. _____ is constantly renewed in the spirit of his mind—having a fresh mental and spiritual attitude: and is putting on the new nature—the regenerate self—created in GOD'S image, GOD-like in true righteousness and holiness.

_____'s life lovingly expresses truth in all things…speaking truly, dealing truly, living truly. _____ is enfolded in love, growing up in every way and in all things unto HIM, Who is the HEAD, even CHRIST, the MESSIAH, the ANOINTED ONE. _____'s mouth will utter Truth of GOD'S Word. _____ speaks excellent and princely things—the opening of his mouth are for right reasons being led by the HOLY SPIRIT. All the words of his mouth are righteous. There is nothing contrary to truth or crooked in them.

_____ inclines his heart to YOUR testimonies, FATHER, and not to covetousness (robbery, sensuality or unworthy riches). _____ does not love or cherish the things in this world above YOU; he counts them as YOUR blessings. The love of the FATHER is in him. He is set free from the lust of the flesh (craving for sensual gratification), the lust of the eyes (greedy longings of the mind) and the pride of life (assurance in his own resources or in the stability of earthly things). _____ perceives and knows the truth and anything false is not from the Truth of GOD'S WORD.

_____ prizes YOUR Wisdom, FATHER, and exalts it, and it will exalt and promote for him as he is attentive to GOD'S Words; consents and submits to YOUR sayings. He keeps them in the center of his heart. For they are life to him and medicine to his whole being. _____ keeps his heart with all diligence, for out of it flow the springs of life.

_____ will do nothing from factional motives through contentiousness, strife, selfishness or for unworthy ends—or prompted by conceit and empty arrogance. Instead, in the true spirit of humility he does regard others as better than he does himself. _____ esteems and looks upon and is concerned for not merely his own interests, but also for the interests of others.

_____ let this same attitude and purpose and humble mind be in him which was in CHRIST JESUS. Thank you, FATHER, in JESUS' Name."

(Keep in mind that Intercession is calling forth those things which are not, as though they were.)

## SCRIPTURE REFERENCES:

Isaiah 54:13  
I John 2:15-16, 21  
Proverbs 8:6-8  
Psalm 119:36  
Ephesians 4:15  
Philippians 2:2-5  
Ephesians 4:23, 24  
Proverbs 4:8, 20-23

# For Those Involved in Court Cases

"FATHER, in the Name of JESUS, it is written in YOUR Word to call on YOU and YOU will answer me and show me great and mighty things. I put YOU in remembrance of YOUR Word and thank YOU that YOU watch over YOUR Word to perform it.

YOUR WORD say that no weapon formed against me will prosper and any tongue that rises against me in judgment will be shown to be wrong. Allow the HOLY SPIRIT to examine my heart that it is in right standing before the FATHER. This peace, security, and triumph over any oppositions are my inheritance as YOUR child. This is the righteousness which I obtain from YOU, FATHER, which YOU imparted with me as YOU have justified me, in the Name of JESUS. I am far from even the thought of destruction, for I will not fear, nor terror will come near me.

FATHER, YOU said YOU will establish me to the end—keep me steadfast, give me strength, and guarantee my vindication; that is, be my warrant against all accusations or indictments. FATHER, YOU contend with those who contend with me and YOUR perfect Works are always concerned to work for my good. I dwell in the secret place of the Most High and this secret place hides me from the strife of tongues for a false witness who breathes out lies is an abomination to YOU.

I am a true witness and all my words are upright and in right standing with YOU, FATHER. By my long forbearing and calmness of spirit, the judge is persuaded and my soft speech breaking down the most bonelike resistance. Therefore, I am not anxious beforehand how I will reply in defense or what I am to say as the HOLY SPIRIT teaches me in that very hour and moment what I ought to say to those in the outside world—my speech is seasoned with salt.

I thank You, FATHER, that Satan and every menacing spirit are bound from operating against me for I am strong in YOU, LORD and in the power of YOUR might, quenching every fiery dart with the Shield of Faith, in JESUS' Name.

Thank YOU, FATHER, that I have increased in YOUR Wisdom, Sature and Ways and I walk in favor with YOU as my GOD and with man. Praise the LORD!"

## SCRIPTURE REFERENCES:

| | | |
|---|---|---|
| Jeremiah 33:3 | Jeremiah 1:12 | Isaiah 43:26 |
| Isaiah 54:17 | Isaiah 54:14 | I Corinthians 1:8 |
| Isaiah 49:25 | Psalm 138:8 | Psalm 91:1 |
| Psalm 31:20 | Proverbs 6:19 | Proverbs 14:25 |
| Proverbs 8:8 | Proverbs 25:15 | Luke 12:11-12 |
| Colossians 4:6 | Matthew 18:18 | Ephesians 6:10, 16 |
| | Luke 2:52 | |

# For Employment

"FATHER, in JESUS' Name, we believe and confess YOUR Word over _____ today knowing that YOU watch over YOUR Word to perform it. YOUR Word prospers in him wherever he is sent; he walks in YOUR favor! FATHER, YOU are his Resource of every consolation, comfort, and encouragement. _____ is courageous and grows in strength.

_____ desires to owe no man anything but to love him. Therefore, _____ is strong and let not his hands become weak or slack, for his work will be rewarded. His wages are not counted as a favor or a gift, but as something owed to him for being diligent in his work. He makes it his ambition and definitely endeavors to live quietly and peacefully, minds his own affairs, and works with his hands and mind to show he bears himself becomingly. He is correct and honorable and commands the respect of the outside world, being self-supporting, but always dependents on GOD alone, and having need of nothing except for YOU, FATHER, Who supplies every need.

He works in quietness, earns works diligently to provide for his own needs, food and other necessities. He is not weary of doing right and continues in well-doing without becoming weary or faint. He learns to apply himself to good deeds—to be an honest and honorable employee—so he is able to meet necessary demands whatever the occasion may require.

FATHER, YOU know the record of _____ works and what he is doing. YOU have set before him a door wide open, which no one is able to shut.

_____ does not fear and is not dismayed for YOU, FATHER, strengthen him. YOU, FATHER, help _____ in JESUS' Name, for in JESUS, _____ has perfect peace and confidence and is of good cheer for JESUS overcame the world—deprived it of its power to harm _____. He does not fret or have anxiety about anything for YOUR Peace, FATHER, mounts guards over his heart and mind. He knows the secret of facing every situation for he is self-sufficient in CHRIST'S sufficiency. He guards his mouth and his tongue keeping himself from trouble.

_____ prizes YOUR Wisdom, FATHER, and acknowledges YOU. YOU direct, make straight and plan his path as YOU promote him. Therefore, FATHER, _____ increases in YOUR wisdom (in broad and full understanding), and in stature and years, and in favor with YOU, FATHER, and with man!"

## SCRIPTURE REFERENCES:

| | | |
|---|---|---|
| Jeremiah 1:12 | Isaiah 55:11 | II Corinthians 1:3 |
| I Corinthians 16:13 | Romans 13:8 | II Chronicles 15:7 |
| Romans 4:4 | I Thessalonians 4:11-12 | Luke 2:52 |
| II Thessalonians 3:12-13 | | Titus 3:14 |
| | Revelation 3:8 | |
| Isaiah 41:10 | John 16:33 | Philippians 4:6-7 |
| Philippians 4:12-13 | Proverbs 21:23 | Proverbs 3:6 |
| | Proverbs 4:8 | |

# For Finding Favor with Others

"FATHER, in the Name of JESUS, YOU make YOUR Face to shine upon and enlighten _____ and are gracious (kind, merciful, and giving favor) to him. _____ is the head and not the tail. He is above only and not beneath.

_____, who seeks YOUR Kingdom and YOUR Righteousness and diligently seeks good, procures favor. He is a blessing to YOU, LORD, and is a blessing to (*name them: family, neighbors, business associates, etc.*). Grace (*favor*) is with those who love the LORD JESUS with a sincere heart and mind. He extends favor, honor and love to (names). He is flowing in YOUR Love, FATHER. YOU are pouring out upon him YOUR Spirit of Favor. YOU crown him with glory and honor for he is YOUR child—YOUR Workmanship.

_____ is a success in YOUR Eyes. He is someone very special with YOU, LORD. He is growing in the LORD—waxing strong in spirit. FATHER, YOU give him knowledge and skill in all learning and wisdom.

YOU bring _____ to find favor, compassion and loving-kindness with (*names*). He obtains favor in the sight of all who look upon him this day in the Name of JESUS. He is filled with YOUR Fullness—rooted and grounded in Love. YOU are doing exceeding abundantly above all that _____ could ever ask or think for YOUR Mighty Power is taking over in _____'s heart and life.

Thank You, FATHER, that _____ is well-favored by YOU and by man, in JESUS' Name!"

## SCRIPTURE REFERENCES:

| | | |
|---|---|---|
| Numbers 6:25 | Deuteronomy 28:13 | Matthew 6:33 |
| Proverbs 11:27 | Ephesians 6:24 | Luke 6:38 |
| Zechariah 12:10 | Psalm 8:5 | Ephesians 2:10 |
| Luke 2:40 | Daniel 1:17, 9 | Esther 2:15, 17 |
| | Ephesians 3:19-20 | |

# For Safety

"FATHER, in the Name of JESUS, I thank YOU that YOU watch over YOUR Word to perform it. I thank YOU that I dwell in the secret place of the Most High and that I remain stable and fixed under the shadow of the Almighty whose Power no enemy can withstand.

FATHER, YOU are my refuge and my fortress. **No evil will befall me—no accident will overtake me—nor will any plague or calamity come near my home.** YOU give YOUR angels special charge over me, to accompany and defend and preserve me in all my ways of obedience and service. They are encamped round about me at all times.

FATHER, YOU are my confidence, firm and strong. YOU keep my foot from being caught in a trap or hidden danger. FATHER, YOU give me safety and ease me—**JESUS is my safety**!

**Traveling**...YOU watch over me in my going out and in my coming in. As I go, I declare YOUR Word, 'Let me arrive and return to my destinations,' since YOUR Word will never return to YOU void, I have those things which I have declared according to YOUR Word. I walk on my way securely with a confident trust; for my heart and mind are firmly fixed and fastened in YOU, and I am kept in perfect peace.

**Sleeping**...FATHER, I sing with Joy upon my bed. When I lay down, my mouth is filled with praise as I acknowledge and thank YOU for the day; always declaring my love for YOU, for YOU continually sustain me. My ear is always sensitive to the Voice of the HOLY SPIRIT throughout the night, always being ready to pray in the spirit for any need you place within my heart and mind. In peace when I lie down and give time to YOU; YOU then give me a full night's sleep, for YOU alone, LORD, cause me to dwell in safety and give me health. I lie down and will not fear for I am guarded from all imaginations that would cause one to worry. My sleep is sweet and peaceful; for YOU give blessings to me even in my sleep. Thank YOU, FATHER, in JESUS' Name. Amen."

*(Continue to feast and meditate upon all of Psalm 91 for yourself and your loved ones!)*

## SCRIPTURE REFERENCES:

| | | |
|---|---|---|
| Jeremiah 1:12 | Psalm 91:1-2 | Psalm 91:10 (*Swedish Translation*) |
| Psalm 91:11 | Psalm 34:7 | Proverbs 3:26 |
| Isaiah 49:25 | Mark 4:35 | Mark 11:23 |
| Proverbs 3:23 | Psalm 112:7 | Isaiah 26:3 |
| Psalm 149:5 | Psalm 3:5 | Psalm 4:8 |
| Proverbs 3:24 | Psalm 127:2 | |

# For Singles Trusting GOD for a Mate

_____ is united to the LORD and has become one spirit with HIM. _____ shuns immorality and all sexual looseness, flees from impurity in thought, word or deed.

_____ knows his body is the temple of the HOLY SPIRIT, Who lives within him, whom _____ has received the Gift of the SPIRIT from GOD. _____ is not his own. _____ was bought for a price, purchased with preciousness, paid for, and made GOD'S own. _____ will honor GOD and bring glory to HIM in his body and in his spirit which are GOD'S.

_____ shuns youthful lusts and flees from them, and aims for and pursues righteousness—all that is virtuous and good, right living, conformity to the Will of GOD in thought, word and deed. He aims at and pursues faith, love, and peace—which are harmony and concord with others—in fellowship with all Christians, who call upon the LORD out of a pure heart.

_____ humbles himself before YOU for whatever might offend YOU, FATHER, or discredits the Name of CHRIST. _____ shows himself to be a blameless, guileless, innocent and an uncontaminated child of GOD without blemish (*faultless*) in the midst of a crooked and wicked generation, among whom _____ is seen as a bright shining Light that clearly discloses darkness in this world, holding out to it and offering to all the Word of Life.

_____ desires to meet the right person that he could love with the Love of CHRIST and to honor and find compatibility and companionship until death due them part. Thank YOU, FATHER, that JESUS is LORD."

## SCRIPTURE REFERENCES:

I Corinthians 6:17-20   Philippians 2:12, 15-16     II Timothy 2:22

# For a Spirit-controlled Life

"The Law of the Spirit of Life in CHRIST JESUS has made _____ free from the law of sin and death. _____'s life is governed not by the standards to the dictates of the flesh, but he is controlled by the HOLY SPIRIT. He is not living the life of the flesh. He is living the Life of the Spirit. The HOLY SPIRIT of GOD dwells within _____ and directs and controls him.

_____ is a conqueror and gains a surpassing victory through JESUS, Who loves him. He does not let himself be overcome by evil, but overcomes and masters evil with good. He has on the Full Armor of Light. He arrays himself with the LORD JESUS CHRIST, the MESSIAH, and makes no provision for indulging the flesh.

_____ is a doer of GOD'S Word. He has GOD'S Wisdom. He is peace-loving, courteous, considerate and gentle, willing to yield to reason, full of compassion, with good fruits. He is free from doubts, wavering, and insincerity. He is subject to GOD.

_____ stands firm against the devil. He resists the devil, and as the devil comes to him one way, and GOD will cause the enemy to flee seven ways. _____ comes close to GOD and GOD comes close to him. _____ does not entertain fear, for GOD never leaves him.

In CHRIST, _____ is filled with the GODHEAD: FATHER, SON, and HOLY SPIRIT. **JESUS is his LORD!"**

## SCRIPTURE REFERENCES:

| | | |
|---|---|---|
| Romans 8:2, 4, 9, 14, 31, 37 | | James 3:17 |
| | Romans 12:21 | |
| Hebrews 13:5 | Romans 13:12, 14 | James 4:7-8 |
| James 1:22 | Colossians 2:10 | |

# For Victory over Fear

"FATHER, in JESUS' Name, I confess and believe that no weapon formed against me will prosper and any tongue that rises against me in judgment will be shown to be in the wrong. I believe I dwell in the secret place of the Most High. I will remain stable and fixed under the shadow of the Almighty GOD, Whose power no enemy can withstand—this secret place hides me from the strife of hurtful tongues.

I believe in the Wisdom of GOD'S Word which dwells in me causing me to realize that I am without fear or dread of evil. In all my ways I know and acknowledge GOD and HIS Word; therefore, HE directs and makes my pathway clear. As I attentively look into GOD'S Word, it brings health to my nerves, mind, and the marrow of my bones.

I am strengthened and reinforced with mighty power in my inner self by the HOLY SPIRIT, Who dwells in me. GOD is my strength and my refuge and I confidently trust in HIM and in HIS Word. I am empowered through my Relationship with Almighty GOD. (This gives me the superhuman, supernatural strength to walk in divine health and to live in HIS abundance.)

***GOD himself has said, I will never leave you without support or forsake you or let you down, my child. I will not, I will not, I will not in any degree leave you helpless or relax my hold on you…assuredly not!***

I take comfort; I'm encouraged; I'm confident and boldly say, ***The LORD is my helper, I will not be seized with alarm, I will not fear or be terrified, for what can man do to me?***

I confess and believe that my children are disciples taught of the LORD and obedient to GOD'S Will. Great is the peace and undisturbed composure are my children—because GOD HIMSELF contends with them the same way HE contends with me; and HE gives them safety and eases them. GOD will perfect that which may concerns my thought as well as my children.

When GOD'S Word is spoken it is alive and full of Power. It is active and operative. It energizes me and it affects me. As I speak GOD'S Word, it is sharper than any Two-edged Sword and it is penetrating into the joints marrow of my bones. It is healing to my flesh. It is prosperity for me. It is the magnificent Word of Almighty GOD. According to HIS Word that I have spoken, so be it! Hallelujah!"

## SCRIPTURE REFERENCES:

| | | |
|---|---|---|
| Isaiah 54:17 | Ephesians 6:10 | Psalm 91:1 |
| Hebrews 13:5-6 | Psalm 31:20 | Isaiah 54:13 |
| Proverbs 3:6, 8 | Isaiah 49:25 | Ephesians 3:16 |
| Psalm 138:8 | Psalm 91:2 | Hebrews 4:12 |

## For Victory Over Gluttony

"FATHER, it is written in YOUR Word that if I confess with my lips that JESUS is LORD and believe in my heart, that YOU have raised HIM from the dead, I declare, 'I am saved.' FATHER, I am YOUR child and confess that JESUS CHRIST is LORD over my spirit, my soul, and my body. I make HIM LORD over every situation in my life. Therefore, I can do all things through CHRIST, Who strengthens me.

FATHER, I make quality decisions to give YOU regarding my appetite. I choose JESUS rather than to the indulgence in the desires of my flesh. I command my body to come in line with YOUR Word. I eat only as much as is sufficient for me. Whenever I eat and I am fully satisfied. ***When I sit down to eat, I consider what is before me.*** I am not given to the desire of over eating and/or eating unhealthy foods.

Like a boxer, I buffet my body—handle it roughly, discipline it by hardships—and subdue it. I bring my body into subjection to my spirit man—the inward man—the real me. Not all things are helpful or good for me to do though permissible. I will not become the slave of anything, or be brought under its power. I do all things in moderation.

My body is the Temple of the HOLY SPIRIT; therefore, I treat it with reverence. I dedicate my body—presenting all my members and faculties—as a living sacrifice, Holy and well pleasing to YOU. I offer or yield myself and my bodily members and faculties to YOU, presenting them as implements of Righteousness. I am united to YOU, LORD, and therefore I am one spirit with YOU. Since my body is the temple, the very sanctuary, of the HOLY SPIRIT, Who lives within me, whom I have received as a Gift from YOU, FATHER; I honor HIM in all that I partake into my body.

I am not my own. I was bought with a price, made to be YOUR own. So therefore, I honor YOU and bring Glory to YOU within my body. Therefore, I always exercise and discipline myself—mortifying my body (deadening my carnal affections, bodily appetites, and worldly desires) endeavoring in all respects—to have a clean (unshaken, blameless) conscience, void of offense toward YOU, FATHER, and toward men. I keep myself from idols—false gods, (from anything and everything that would occupy the place in my heart due to serving YOU with a whole heart, from any sort of substitute; for YOU are have the first place in my life).

I no longer spend the rest of my natural life living by my human appetites and desires, but I live for what YOU Will! I am on my guard. I walk in health. I refuse to be overburdened and depressed, weighed down with dizziness, headaches, nausea of self-indulgence, drunkenness (on food), worldly worries and cares, for I have been given a Spirit of Power and of Love and of Calm and Well-balanced Mind and disciplined by the Word and have self-control.

FATHER, I do resist temptation, in the Name of JESUS. I strip off and throw aside every encumbrance—unnecessary weight—and the spirit of gluttony has no dominion over my body, nor shall it try to cling to or entangle me. I run with patient, endurance, being steady and active persistence the appointed course of the race that is set before me, looking away from all that will distract me from JESUS, the Author, and the Finisher of my faith.

CHRIST, the MESSIAH, will be **magnified** and receive **glory** and **praise** in this body which was given to me to be Holy and will boldly be **exalted** within my person. Thank you, FATHER, in JESUS' Name! Hallelujah!"

## SCRIPTURE REFERENCES:

| | | |
|---|---|---|
| Romans 10:9-10 | Philippians 4:13 | Deuteronomy 30:19 |
| Romans 13:14 | Proverbs 25:16 | I Corinthians 6:12-13, 17 |
| Proverbs 23:1-3 | Romans 6:13 | I Corinthians 9:27 |
| I Corinthians 6:19-20 | Romans 12:1 | Luke 21:34 |
| II Timothy 1:7 | James 4:7 | Hebrews 12:1-2 |
| | Philippians 1:20 | |

# For Health and Healing

"FATHER, in the Name of JESUS, we confess YOUR Word concerning YOUR Divine Healing. As we do this, we believe and say that YOUR Word will not return to YOU void, but it will accomplish what YOUR Promises declare according to YOUR Will. Therefore, we believe, in the Name of JESUS, that _____ is healed according to I Peter 2:24. It is written in YOUR Word that JESUS HIMSELF took our infirmities and bore our sicknesses. (Matthew 8:17.) Therefore, with great boldness and confidence we say on the Authority of YOUR written Word that _____ is redeemed from the curse of sickness and refuses to tolerate any and all symptoms."

"SATAN, WE SPEAK TO YOU, IN THE NAME OF JESUS, AND SAY THAT YOUR PRINCIPALITIES, POWERS, YOUR MASTER SPIRITS WHO RULE THE PRESENT DARKNESS, AND YOUR SPIRITUAL WICKNEDNESS IN HEAVENLY PLACES ARE BOUND FROM OPERATING AGAINST _____ IN ANY WAY. AS GOD ALMIGHTY'S INTERCESSORS, WE DECLARE _____ IS LOOSENED AND FREED FROM YOUR ASSIGNMENT. _____ IS THE PROPERTY OF ALMIGHTY GOD AND WE GIVE YOU NO PLACE IN ANY PART OF THE PHYSICAL BODY AND MIND, SINCE YOU CAN IN NO WAY TAMPER WITH THE SPIRIT, OF _____. _____ DWELLS IN THE SECRET PLACE OF THE MOST HIGH GOD; AND ABIDES,

REMAINS STABLE, AND FIXED UNDER THE SHADOW OF THE ALMIGHTY, WHO'S POWER NO FOE CAN WITHSTAND."

"Now, FATHER, because we reverence and worship YOU, we have assurance of YOUR Word that the angels of the LORD are encamped around _____ and delivers *him* from every evil work. No evil will befall *him*, no plague or calamity will come near his dwelling place. We confess that the Word of GOD abides in _____ and delivers *him* with the Peace of GOD, having a sound mind, and having the wholeness in body and spirit from the deepest parts of *his* nature in *his* immortal spirit even to the joints and marrow of *his* bones. We declare that YOUR Word is medication and life to *his* flesh for the Law of the Spirit of Life operates in _____ and makes *him* free from the law of sin and death.

We declare over _____ that in weakness of the physical body *he* still remains wearing the Whole Armor of GOD, and is continually protected with the Shield of Faith from all the fiery darts of the wicked one. JESUS is the High Priest of our confession, and we hold fast to our confession of faith in YOUR Word. We stand immovable and fixed in the full assurance that _____ is set free from any form of infirmity and has complete health, NOW, in the Name of JESUS. From this time forward we continually thank YOU, FATHER, in JESUS Name, that this is DONE. We also declare the peace that passes all understanding and "**Do not walk by sight, but by faith according to YOUR Word.**" We, also declare if the spirit of worry would overcome anyone around him, the HOLY SPIRIT will rebuke them and convince them to become immovable in their work of faith. Satan is a defeated foe! Hallelujah! Amen!"

## SCRIPTURE REFERENCES:

| | | |
|---|---|---|
| Isaiah 55:11 | II Timothy 1:7 | Galatians 3:13 |
| Hebrews 4:12, 14 | James 4:7 | Proverbs 4:22 |
| Ephesians 6:12 | Romans 8:2 | II Corinthians 10:4 |
| Ephesians 6:11, 16 | Psalm 91:1, 10 | Psalm 112:7 |
| | Psalm 34:7 | |

# For Unknown Types of Diseases and Cancer

"FATHER, in the Name of JESUS, we confess YOUR Word concerning YOUR Divine Healing and that YOU are the Omniscient and Omnipotent GOD. We also declare that Wisdom only comes from YOU and we acknowledge that the professional people in this world who lack humility, will come to know YOUR Powers are Mighty, for they too will come to acknowledge in YOUR GODLY Gift of Wisdom and Knowledge, for they too will come to know through YOU all things are possible. We also declare in every situation that YOUR Word will not return to YOU void, but it will accomplish what YOUR Promises declare to accomplish according to YOUR Will. Therefore, we believe in the Name of JESUS, healing is ours as children of GOD according to I Peter 2:24. It is written in YOUR Word that JESUS; HIMSELF took our infirmities and bore our sicknesses. (Matthew 8:17.) Therefore, with great boldness and confidence we say on the Authority of YOUR Written Word that we are redeemed from the curse of sickness and refuse to tolerate any and all symptoms. We acknowledge that man's immortal mind is incapable to know all things. Therefore, we NOW declare that Medical Physicians and Researchers, all medical treatments are anointed by the Power of GOD and will perform according to GOD'S Word. Through the anointing of YOUR children with unknown diseases and illnesses brought forth by the enemy are defeated, because YOUR HOLY DIVINE Presence resides in us, through JESUS CHRIST. YOUR Anointing within YOUR children will enlighten or open the minds of all Medical staff with YOUR Divine Knowledge and Wisdom will be revealed as they examine our bodies.

We remind YOU, FATHER, GOD, YOUR angel of the LORD, which you put in Balaam's pathway; Balaam's two servants witness this event. The donkey saw the angel of the LORD standing with HIS Sword drawn in HIS Hand, YOU used the donkey by opening its mouth and spoke to Balaam rebuking him for being so ignorant. You then opened Balaam's eyes, and he saw the angel of the LORD standing in the way with the drawn sword (*the sword represents the Word of GOD*). Balaam humbled himself and did according to the Word of the angel of the LORD. According to YOUR Word and in JESUS Name, I declare that YOUR Word goes forcefully into the minds of the most stubborn minds of people within the Medical and their Researchers world (including drug corporations) to walk in YOUR Wisdom and Knowledge disclosing any unknown disease or illness."

"THEREFORE, SATAN, WE SPEAK TO YOU, IN THE NAME OF JESUS, AND SAY THAT YOUR PRINCIPALITIES, POWERS, YOUR MASTER SPIRITS WHO RULE IN THIS PRESENT DARKNESS, AND YOUR SPIRITUAL WICKNEDNESS IN HEAVENLY PLACES ARE BOUND FROM OPERATING AND TAMPERING WITH GOD'S CREATION. WE THWART YOUR WORKS FROM DISTORTING AND/OR MUTATING THE CELLS THAT GOD HAS CREATED WITHIN US IN ANY WAY. AS GOD ALMIGHTY'S INTERCESSORS, WE BIND YOUR WORKS OF DARKNESS, DESTROYING OUR GOD GIVEN CELLS, AND WE LOOSEN GOD'S WORD AND ARE FREE YOU FROM

YOUR ASSIGNMENT. WE ARE THE PROPERTY OF ALMIGHTY GOD AND WE GIVE YOU NO PLACE IN ANY PART OUR PHYSICAL BODY, SPIRIT, AND MIND. FOR WE DWELL IN THE SECRET PLACE OF THE MOST HIGH GOD; AND WE ABIDE, REMAINING STABLE, AND FIXED UNDER THE SHADOW OF THE ALMIGHTY, WHO'S POWER NO ENEMY CAN WITHSTAND."

"Now, FATHER, because we reverence and worship YOU, we have the assurance of YOUR Word that the angels of the LORD encamps around YOUR children and deliver *us* from every evil work. No evil will befall *us*, no plague or calamity will come near our dwelling place. We confess that the Word of GOD abides within *us* and delivers *us* with the peace of GOD, having a sound mind, and having the wholeness in body and spirit from the deepest parts of *our* nature in *our* immortal spirit even to the joints and marrow of *our* bones. We declare that YOUR Word is medication and life to *our* flesh for the Law of the Spirit of Life operates within *us* and has set *us* free from the law of sin and death.

We declare even in weakness of the physical body, *we* Spiritually STAND Strong, wearing the Whole Armor of GOD; and we are protected with the Shield of Faith from all the fiery darts of the wicked one. JESUS is the High Priest of our confession, and we hold fast to our confession of faith according to YOUR Word. We stand immovable and fixed in the full assurance that we walk with have health and our health has been GOD'S Perfect Plan for our lives, NOW, in the Name of JESUS. From this time forward we continually thank YOU, FATHER, in JESUS Name that this is DONE. We also declare the peace that passes all understanding and "**Do Not walk by sight, but by faith according to YOUR Word.**" We also declare if the spirit of worry overcomes us; the HOLY SPIRIT will rebuke the spirit of worry and convince us to be immovable in our work of faith. Satan is a defeated foe! Hallelujah! Amen!

## SCRIPTURE REFERENCES:

| | | |
|---|---|---|
| Isaiah 55:11 | II Timothy 1:7 | Galatians 3:13 |
| Hebrews 4:12, 14 | James 4:7 | Proverbs 4:22 |
| Numbers 22: 22-35 | II Peter 2: 15-16 | Ephesians 6:12 |
| Romans 8:2 | II Corinthians 10:4 | Ephesians 6:11, 16 |
| Psalm 91:1, 10 | Psalm 112:7 | Psalm 34:7 |

# Intercession for the Handicapped

"FATHER, we come before you boldly and confidently knowing that YOU shall not lie and that YOU watch over YOUR Word to perform it. Therefore, FATHER, we bring before YOU those who are called handicapped and ill—mentally and physically. FATHER, by the Authority of YOUR Word, we know without a doubt that it is YOUR will for these people—babies, children, and adults—to be made completely whole and restored in the Name of JESUS; for we know it to be YOUR Will. YOU will never give us more than we can handle.

We know, FATHER, that Satan, the god of this world, comes against YOUR Handiwork. But we also know that YOU are the GOD of Miracles, the GOD of Love, with Power and Might. Through YOUR Redemptive Plan, what JESUS did on the Cross and in the pit of hell for us we, YOUR people, are redeemed from the curse of the law. The Law of the Spirit of Life in CHRIST JESUS has set us free from the law of sin and death. We are seated with CHRIST in Heavenly places far above all satanic forces.

So we bring these people before YOUR throne of Grace, who have been attacked mercilessly — mentally and physically — by Satan and his cohorts. We intercede in behalf for them and their families and loved ones."

"SATAN, WE SPEAK TO YOU AND TO THE PRINCIPALITIES, POWERS, RULERS OF THE DARKNESS IN THIS WORLD, AND WICKED SPIRITS IN HEAVENLY PLACES,

AND WE BIND YOU AND LOOSEN YOU FROM YOUR ASSIGNMENTS AGAINST THESE PEOPLE IN THE MIGHTY NAME OF THE LORD JESUS. YOU CAN NO LONGER HARASS OR HINDER THESE PEOPLE WHO HAVE THE OPPORTUNITY THIS DAY TO MAKE JESUS THEIR LORD AND SAVIOR. WE BIND DOUBT, UNBELIEF, FEAR, TRADITION, DISCOURAGEMENT, DEPRESSION AND OPPRESSION FROM OPERATING AGAINST THE PARENTS, CHILDREN, AND INDIVIDUALS INVOLVED; LOOSEN YOUR POWERFUL WORK AND PROMISES TO FILL THESE PARENTS, CHILDREN, AND INDIVIDUALS INVOLVED."

"FATHER, we pray for born-again, SPIRIT-filled people in positions of Authority—administrators, teachers, doctors, nurses, orderlies, attendants, and volunteers to come forth in giving aid to them. We pray that men and women of integrity, blameless and complete in YOUR sight, remain in these positions, but that the wicked be cut off and the treacherous be rooted out. FATHER, we pray for laborers of the harvest to go forth preaching the Good News to the lost and to edify the Body of CHRIST. We pray that YOU quicken these people to YOUR Word—that they will be filled with Wisdom and Revelation Knowledge concerning the integrity of YOUR Word, speaking faith-filled words and responding as faith-filled Believers, having the infilling of the HOLY SPIRIT, Divine Health, the fruit of the recreated human Spirit, the Gifts of the HOLY SPIRIT, and Deliverance. May each individual know that JESUS is their Source of every consolation, comfort, and encouragement and that through HIM they are to be sanctified in Spirit, Mind, and Body.

We confess that they are redeemed from the curse of the law—redeemed from every sickness, disease, malady, affliction, defect, deficiency, deformity, injury, and every demon.

We speak healing to unborn infants in the wombs of mothers for, *Lo children are a heritage from the LORD, the fruit of the womb a reward, and blessed.*

We speak restoration to damaged brain cells and the activation of dormant brain cells. We speak normal intellect for one's age. We speak creative miracles to the parts of the body. We speak healing to all wounds. We speak words of Life and say that you will live in victory in this life and never spiritually die. We declare perfect soundness of mind and wholeness in body and spirit. We say that tongues are loosed and our speech is distinct. We say, ears, you hear and eyes, you see, in the Name of JESUS. We say demons are cast out bowing to the Name of JESUS. We speak deliverance to bodies and minds, for YOU, LORD GOD, are the help of their countenance and the lifter of those bowed down—the Joy of the LORD is their strength and stronghold!

We commission GOD'S ministering spirits to go forth as they obey GOD'S Word to provide the necessary help for and assistance to those we are praying for!

FATHER, no Word of Yours is void of the power that it takes to cause itself to come to pass! We establish YOUR Word on this earth for it is already forever settled in Heaven. Nothing is too hard or impossible for YOU. All things are possible to those who believe. We pray for more intercessors to stand with us. Let our prayers be set forth as incense before YOU—as sweet fragrance unto YOU! Praise be to the LORD GOD Almighty!"

## SCRIPTURE REFERENCES:

| | | |
|---|---|---|
| Romans 3:4 | Jeremiah 1:12 | Acts 3:16 |
| II Corinthians 4:4 | John 10:10 | Galatians 3:13 |
| Romans 8:2 | Ephesians 2:6 | Matthew 18:18 |
| Proverbs 2:21-22 | Mark 16:17 | Psalm 42:11 |
| Psalm 146:8 | Nehemiah 8:10 | Psalm 103:20 |
| Matthew 9:37-38 | Ephesians 1:17-18 | II Corinthians 1:3 |
| I Thessalonians 5:23 | Psalm 127:3 | Mark 11:23-24 |
| I Peter 2:24 | Matthew 8:17 | Mark 7:35 |
| Proverbs 20:12 | Luke 1:37 | Psalm 119:89 |
| Jeremiah 32:27 | Mark 9:23 | Psalm 141:2 |

# For Children and Parents

"FATHER, in the Name of JESUS, I pray and confess YOUR Word over my children and surround them with YOUR measure of faith—faith that comes from YOUR Word that YOU watch over them to perform it! I confess and believe that my children are Disciples of Christ; taught by the HOLY SPIRIT and obedient to YOUR Will. Great is the peace and undisturbed behavior of my children...because YOU GOD, protect them and cause them to achieve even when a contender attempts to thwart the walk of my children and YOU provide safety them for them, peace and comfort them. For YOUR angels continually encamp round about them.

FATHER, YOU will perfect that which concerns me. *I commit and cast the care of my children once and for all, over onto YOU, FATHER.* They are in YOUR Hands, and I am positively persuaded that YOU are more than able to guard and keep that which I have committed to YOU. **YOU are more than enough!**

I confess that my children obey their parents in the LORD as HIS Representatives for this is just and right. My children _____ honor, esteem, and value their parents; for this is the first commandment with a promise: that all may be well with my children and that they may live a long life on earth. I believe and confess that my children will choose YOU to be their LORD and to love YOU with their whole heart. LORD they will listen and hear YOUR Voice as they learn to obey YOUR Ways, and cling to YOU; for YOU are their life and the length of their days. Therefore, my children are the head and not the tail and will be above only and not beneath and are blessed in their going out and coming in or where ever they may be, YOUR presence will always be with them and the HOLY SPIRIT will always convince them to make good decisions.

I believe and confess that YOU give YOUR angels charge over my children to accompany and defend and preserve them in all their ways. YOU, LORD, are their refuge and fortress and have made them to be leaders and not given into their peers as followers. YOU are their glory and the lifter of their heads.

As parents, we will not provoke, irritate, or frustrate our children. When they are young we will rightly impart YOUR Principles and Standards with love. We will be strict with them but with loving kindness. In no way we will harass them, or cause them to become discouraged, sullen, gloomy, ill-tempered and feel inferior and frustrated. We will not break or wound their spirit, but we will rear them tenderly in the training, discipline, counsel, and admonition of the LORD. We will train them in the way they should go and when they are older is when we see the fruit of our labor and see that they have not departed from YOUR Ways.

Oh, LORD, my LORD, how excellent (*majestic and glorious*) is YOUR Name in all the earth! YOU have set YOUR Glory on or above the Heavens. Out of the mouth of babes and un-weaned infants YOU have established strength because of their foes, that YOU will silence the enemy and the avenger. I sing praise to YOUR Name, Oh Most High.

The enemy is turned back from my children, in the Name of JESUS! _____ shall increase in wisdom and in favor with GOD and man."

## SCRIPTURE REFERENCES:

| | | |
|---|---|---|
| Jeremiah 1:12 | Isaiah 54:13 | Isaiah 49:25 |
| I Peter 5:7 | II Timothy 1:12 | Ephesians 6:1-3 |
| Deuteronomy 30:19-20, 3, 6 | Psalm 91:11, 2 | Deuteronomy 28:13, |
| Psalm 3:3 | Colossians 3:21 | Ephesians 6:4 |
| Proverbs 22:6 | Psalm 8:1-2 | Psalm 9:2-3 |
| | Luke 2:52 | |

# For the Home

"FATHER, I thank YOU that YOU have blessed our home and family with all spiritual blessings in CHRIST JESUS.

Through skillful and GODLY wisdom my life and family ("our home") are steadfastly built, and by understanding it is established on a sound and good foundation by having Daily Devotions. For by YOUR knowledge our home will be blessed (in every area) being filled with all precious and pleasant riches — great priceless memories. The house of the uncompromisingly righteous will stand. Prosperity and welfare are in our home, in the Name of JESUS.

Our home is securely built. It is founded on the Rock of JESUS—having Revelation Knowledge from YOUR Word, FATHER. JESUS is the Cornerstone of our home. JESUS is LORD of our household; HE is LORD of our home—spirit, mind, and within our bodies.

Whatever may be our task we will do it with our whole hearts as something done for YOU, LORD, and not for men. We love each other with GOD'S Perfect Love, and we dwell in peace. This home is deposited into YOUR charge, entrusted to YOUR protection and watched over by YOUR angels encamped round about this property.

**FATHER, as for me and my house we will serve the LORD, in JESUS' name. Hallelujah!"**

## SCRIPTURE REFERENCES:

| | | |
|---|---|---|
| Ephesians 1:3 | Proverbs 24:3-4 | Proverbs 15:6 |
| Proverbs 12:7 | Psalm 112:3 | Luke 6:48 |
| Acts 4:11 | Acts 16:31 | Philippians 2:10-11 |
| Colossians 3:23 | Colossians 3:14-15 | Acts 20:32 |
| | Joshua 24:15 | |

# For Our Mates

"FATHER, in the Name of JESUS, I take YOUR Word and confess this day that my mate may listen with obedience to the Wisdom of GOD and that he and I will dwell securely and in confident trust and learn to be quiet to hear the Voice of the HOLY SPIRIT without any interruption from the enemy, nor by any spirit of fear or dread of evil. _____ makes his ear attentive to skillful and GODLY Wisdom, and inclines and directs his heart and mind to understanding. He applies all of HIS Power to the quest of it.

He trusts in the LORD with HIS mercy, kindness, and truth, for he knows GOD will never forsake him. He meditates upon YOUR Word and allows the HOLY SPIRIT to inscribe the Word within his heart and mind. He highly prizes the Wisdom of GOD and exalts her (*wisdom*). Wisdom and Understanding will exalt and promote him—it will bring him honor because he has embraced GOD'S Wisdom and Understanding deep within his inner being. For the LORD is his confidence, firm and strong and will keep his foot from being caught in a trap or any hidden danger.

Wherever he goes, the Word or Wisdom of GOD will lead him. When he sleeps, it will keep him. When he wakes, he will acknowledge HIM. Therefore, he will speak excellent and princely things and the opening of his lips will be for right things. All the words of his mouth are righteous—upright and in Right Standing with GOD—and there is nothing contrary to truth or crooked in them.

_____ will live considerately with me—with an intelligent recognition of our relationship. Honor and respect is as the crown of gold in our home. However, he does realize that we are joint heirs to the Throne with JESUS. He does this in order that our prayers will not be hindered or cut off.

I confess that we are one and of the same mind, united in spirit, compassionate and courteous, tenderhearted and humble-minded. I believe for our welfare, happiness, and protection because we love and respect each other.

"Thank you, FATHER, that my mate for life, is of good report, he is successful in everything he sets his hand to do. He is uncompromisingly righteous. He captures human lives for GOD as a fisher of men. As he does this, he has the confidence that YOU are the LORD GOD who teaches him to profit and leads him in the way he should go; abundantly supplied knowing every need is met! He has obtained the favor of the LORD and the Will of GOD is done in his life!"

## SCRIPTURE REFERENCES:

| | | |
|---|---|---|
| Proverbs 1:33 | Proverbs 2:2 | Proverbs 3:3 |
| Proverbs 4:8 | Proverbs 3:26 | Proverbs 6:22 |
| Proverbs 8:6-8 | I Peter 3:7-9 | Proverbs 11:30 |
| | Isaiah 48:17 | |

# For a Harmonious Relationship (Union)

"FATHER, in the Name of JESUS, it's written in YOUR Word that love is shed abroad in our hearts by the HOLY SPIRIT, Who is given to us. Because YOU dwell within us, we acknowledge that love reigns supreme. We believe that love is displayed in full expression enfolding the compatibility of knitting the two together as one, making us perfect for every good work to do YOUR Will, working in and through us which is pleasing in YOUR Sight.

We live and conduct ourselves with honor and example. We esteem it as precious, worthy and of great price. We commit ourselves to live in mutual harmony and one accord, delighting in one another, being of the same mind and united in our spirits.

FATHER, we believe and say that we are gentle, compassionate, courteous, tender-hearted and humble-minded. We seek peace and it keeps our hearts in quietness and assurance. Because we follow after love and dwell in peace, our prayers are not hindered in any way, in the Name of JESUS. We are heirs together by the Grace of GOD.

Our union grows stronger day by day in the bond of unity because it is grounded within YOUR Word and also rooted and grounded in YOUR Love that drives out the enemy from our home. FATHER, we thank YOU for the performance of the working of YOUR Word, in JESUS' Name."

## SCRIPTURE REFERENCES:

| | | |
|---|---|---|
| Romans 5:5 | Ephesians 4:32 | Philippians 1:9 |
| Isaiah 32:17 | Colossians 3:14 | Philippians 4:7 |
| Colossians 1:10 | I Peter 3:7 | Philippians 2:13 |
| Ephesians 3:17-18 | Philippians 2:2 | Jeremiah 1:12 |

# For Compatibility in the Home (Union)

"FATHER, in the Name of JESUS, I pray and confess that (*name both names*) endure long and are patient and kind; that we are never envious and never boil over with jealousy. That we both function with the fruits of the SPIRIT and especially of self-control, that we never give room for the spirit of anger. We are not boastful or vainglorious and we do not display ourselves haughtily. We are not conceited or arrogant and inflated with pride. We are not rude and unmannerly towards each other, but set our goal to be in harmony. We do not insist on our own rights or our own way for we are not self-seeking or fretful or resentful. We take no account of the evil done to us and pay no attention to a suffered wrong. We do not rejoice at injustice and unrighteousness, but we rejoice when right and truth prevails.

We bear up under anything and everything that comes our way. We are ever ready to believe the best of each other. Our hopes are fadeless under all circumstances. We endure everything without weakening. OUR LOVE NEVER FAILS—it never fades out or becomes obsolete or comes to an end.

We are confessing that our lives and our family's lives lovingly express truth in all things. We speak truly, deal truly, and live truly. We are enfolded in love; we live and learn and mature through all our experiences. We esteem and delight in one another, forgiving one another readily and free each other, as CHRIST has forgiven us. We are imitators of GOD and copies of HIS example of love for HIS children.

Thank YOU, FATHER, that our union grows stronger each day because it is founded upon YOUR Word and on YOUR kind of Love. We give YOU ALL the praise for it, FATHER, in the Name of JESUS."

## SCRIPTURE REFERENCES:

I Corinthians 13:4-8   Ephesians 4:15, 32   I Corinthians 14:1
                       Ephesians 5:1-2

# Intercession for a Troubled Relationships

"FATHER, in the Name of JESUS, we bring _____ before YOU. We pray and confess YOUR Word over them, and as we do, we use our faith, believing that YOUR Word will work mightily within them, as it comes to pass.

Therefore we pray and confess that _____ will let go of all bitterness, indignation, wrath, passion, rage, bad tempers, resentment, brawling, clamor, contention and slander, evil speaking, abusive, and blasphemous language be banished from them; also all malice, spite, ill will or disharmony of any kind...that _____ will become helpful, useful, kind and loving towards each other, tenderhearted, compassionate, understanding, having a loving heart, forgiving one another readily and freely calling upon YOU as their FATHER; so they will put on the mind of CHRIST, forgave each other, just as JESUS has forgiven them. Therefore, _____ will be imitators of YOU, GOD. They will copy YOU by following YOUR example of loved children as they imitate their FATHER. _____ will walk in love, esteeming and desire to delight in one another as CHRIST loved them and gave HIMSELF up for them, as a slain offering and sacrifice to YOU GOD, so their lives will become a sweet fragrance unto YOU."

"SATAN, WE RENDER YOU HELPLESS IN YOUR ACTIVITIES IN THE LIVES OF _____, AND COME AGAINST YOUR SPIRIT OF THE THOUGHT OR

TEMPTATION OF SEPARATION OR DIVORCE. WE LOOSE YOU FROM YOUR ASSIGNMENT AGAINST THEM. SATAN, YOUR POWER IS BROKEN FROM HINDERING THEIR UNION, IN THE NAME OF JESUS."

"FATHER, we thank YOU that _____ will constantly be renewed in their spirits and their minds having a fresh mental and spiritual attitude. They have put on the Nature of CHRIST, for they are created in GOD'S Image in true Righteousness and Holiness. They have come to their senses having escaped out from under the snare of the devil, who has tried to hold them captive, but from this point forward we call YOUR Word to be accomplished, which is to love one another with the GOD Kind of love united in total peace and harmony and happiness.

Thank YOU for the answer, LORD. We know it is done NOW, in the Name of JESUS."

## SCRIPTURE REFERENCES:

Ephesians 4:31-32　　Ephesians 4:23-24　　Ephesians 5:1-2
II Timothy 2:26　　　Matthew 18:18

# For the 100-fold Return

"FATHER, in JESUS' Name, I give honor to the truth and integrity of YOUR Word. I thank YOU for the 100-fold return as I give cheerfully unto YOU. I confess before YOU and all the host of Heaven and earth that the 100-fold return is mine according to YOUR Word. I have given of my life and possessions to follow YOU. I have given for the Gospel's sake. Now I know the full 100-fold return is working its way as it is coming into my life. I confess that YOU are causing it to come to me in abundance. It belongs to me. ***YOUR Word says it is mine, so I say it is mine.*** I have it, in JESUS' Name. Amen!

I receive the abundance of life. I receive YOUR blessings. It is YOU, Who gave me the Power through the Blood of JESUS and the Power of the HOLY SPIRIT to receive wealth that YOU have establish in YOUR Covenant for me. I thank YOU for the Revelation Knowledge of that Covenant which is steadily increasing within my spirit. The Word of GOD is True, and I know that YOU are alert and active, watching over YOUR Word to perform it in my life.

FATHER, I am thankful that the blessings of the LORD make me truly rich in wealth, knowledge and wisdom and as YOU may use any form of sorrow, I have the assurance YOU will always turn it for my good. The loving-kindness and tender mercies of the LORD endure forever. Goodness and mercy are mine all the days of my life, in JESUS' Name. Amen. So be it! Praise the LORD!"

## SCRIPTURE REFERENCES:

| | | |
|---|---|---|
| Mark 10:29-30 | Jeremiah 1:9-12, 19 | Mark 11:23 |
| Proverbs 10:22 | Deuteronomy 8:18 | Deuteronomy 30:19 |
| Colossians 1:10 | Psalm 23:6 and 1 *("...I will not want")* | |

# Prosperity for You and Others

"FATHER, in the Name of YOUR SON, JESUS, we confess YOUR Word over _____ this day. As we do this, we say it with our mouths and believe it in our hearts and know that YOUR Word will not return to YOU void, but will accomplish what it says it will do.

Therefore, we believe in the Name of JESUS that _____'s needs are met according to Philippians 4:19. We believe that because of YOUR Promises; _____ have cheerfully been given to further YOUR cause, gifts will be given to him, in good measure, pressed down, shaken together and running over will they pour into his bosom. For with the measure he deals out, it will be measured back to him. FATHER, we confess a hundredfold return for him according to Mark 10:29-30.

FATHER, YOU have delivered _____ out of the authority of darkness into the Kingdom of YOUR Dear SON. FATHER, we believe _____ knows he is YOUR child. We confess YOU have assumed YOUR place as his FATHER and have made YOUR home to be with him. You are taking care of him and even now enabling him to walk in love and in wisdom, and to walk in the fullness of fellowship with YOUR SON."

"SATAN, WE BIND YOU FROM _____'S FINANCES AND FROM YOUR ASSIGNMENT AGAINST HIM, ACCORDING TO MATTHEW

18:18 AND LOOSE GOD'S RICHES TO BE POURED INTO HIS LIFE."

"We thank YOU, for the ministering Spirits which YOU have given to him are now freed to minister for _____ and bring in the necessary finances.

FATHER, we confess that YOU are a very present help in trouble, and YOU are more than enough. We confess, GOD, YOU are able to make all grace, every favor and earthly blessing, to flow into his life in abundance; so that he is always and in all circumstances and whatever the need, self-sufficient, possessing enough to require no aid or support and furnished in abundance for every good work and charitable donation."

## SCRIPTURE REFERENCES:

| | | |
|---|---|---|
| Isaiah 55:11 | II Corinthians 6:16, 18 | Philippians 4:19 |
| Matthew 18:18 | Luke 6:38 | Hebrews 1:14 |
| Mark 10:29-30 | II Corinthians 9:8 | Colossians 1:13 |
| | Psalm 46:1 | |

# A Dedication for Your Tithes

"We profess this day unto the LORD GOD that we have come into the inheritance which the LORD swore to give us. We are in the land which YOU have provided for us in JESUS CHRIST, the Kingdom of Almighty GOD. We called upon YOU, in the Name of JESUS and have made YOU to be LORD of our lives; YOU heard our cry and delivered us into the Kingdom of YOUR Dear SON.

JESUS, as our LORD and High priest, for by faith may we learned to bring the first fruits of our income to YOU, as worship to the LORD our GOD with joy, adoration and thanksgiving.

We recognize that bringing forth our tithe unto to YOU is an "**Act of Faith**," which YOU honor and give great rewards that are over flowing with YOUR blessings. But we also acknowledge that it is a learning process to give a tenth of our income and we know YOUR Grace is there to help us learn to respond to YOUR Word accurately. We ask that as YOU teach us to use our faith in doing so, that we will know it is a true Joy to bring our tithe into your storehouse; but as people, in this world, who are financially struggling to meet their own needs, this is a "**big**" step of faith to accomplish on their part. We need the help of the HOLY SPIRIT to show us the importance with Understanding and Wisdom; and we need YOUR patience as we learn to work our faith to become a "**cheerful giver**." We know the working of our faith will receive and see YOUR rewards come back quickly to us as we are taking that step of faith. Then as we grow in learning to be diligent in bringing our tithes to YOUR storehouse, it will then be easy to also give our offerings to others who are in need. We also acknowledge that a "**True Tither**" is also one who freely gives offerings over and above their tithes. YOU are always pleased when YOUR children work their faith and learn to give with a cheerful heart. We know that we are never to give out of obligation, for that is an act which YOU cannot honor; for YOU only desire people who give cheerfully without fear and with total faith, knowing that YOU will always meet all of their needs.

We rejoice in all the blessings YOU have given to us and within our household. As we have listened to the Voice of the LORD, our GOD, and have done according to all that YOU have commanded us. Now look down from YOUR Holy Habitation, from Heaven, and bless us as YOU Promised in YOUR Word. We thank YOU, FATHER, in JESUS' Name."

## SCRIPTURE REFERENCES:
Deuteronomy 26: 1, 3, 10-11, 14-15    Colossians 1:13
Ephesians 2:1-5    Hebrews 3:1, 7-8

# References

All Scripture references are taken from either:
*The King James Version, The New King James Version, The International Version, the New Amplified Bible and the Classic Edit of the Amplified Bible.*

Adams, Billie– *"Dynamic Prayer Power"*

Capps, Charles– *"Prayer that Changes Things"*

Copeland, Gloria– *"GOD'S Will for You"*

Copeland, Kenneth – *"Believer's Voice of Victory"* and *"GOD'S Plan for Your Life"*

Hagin, Kenneth – *"Man on Three Dimensions"* and *"Praying to Get Result"* and *"Faith Food"*

Kenyon, E. W. – *"In His Presence"*

The Amplified Bible (King James Version)

The Swedish Version Bible

# Notes:

| Dates & Notes to Answered Pray: |
|---|
|  |
|  |
|  |
|  |
|  |
|  |
|  |
|  |
|  |
|  |
|  |
|  |
|  |

**Dates & Notes to answered Pray:**

**Dates & Notes to answered Pray:**

**General Notes:**

**General Notes:**

**General Notes:**

www.ingramcontent.com/pod-product-compliance
Lightning Source LLC
LaVergne TN
LVHW061545070526
838199LV00077B/6914